Original KNITTING and Crochet for Babies

Lyric Books Limited

© 1995 Lyric Books Limited
Central House, 7-8 Ritz Parade, Western Avenue, London W5 3RA England

ISBN 0 7111 0092 6

Printed in Spain

Introduction

We were in the garden having a drink. Julia Carpenter had just mentioned that she had become a grandmother for the first time. She was talking with enthusiasm about knitting again after a gap of 20 years.

'I publish books on knitting and crochet,' I said. As a sporting philistine, it was a statement which drew a smile and the normal incredulous response. Julia, however, who was to become the inspiration for this book, continued; 'Well, I can tell you that there is not a decent baby knitting book in any bookshop or specialist knitting yarn shop. It is impossible to find any original patterns or ideas. I've looked everywhere. There's nothing!'

Research indicated that Julia was correct. Baby knitting and pattern books have practically disappeared. Those that were found were very dated. Some that were still on sale had been published first as 'traditional' books in the 1960's! I called Julia, who was keen, as a young grandmother, to create a personal wardrobe for her new granddaughter. After a layoff of twenty years the needles were to click again. None of the skill had disappeared and she experienced an immediate bonding and satisfaction from her labour as she knitted.

She discovered that it was more rewarding and less expensive to knit than to shop. Simply selecting from the 'ready mades' in the High Street was impersonal and boring. They were, she found, expensive, overpriced, cheaply knitted and poor value. She had decided that her granddaughter was going to have original knits in unique colour combinations. She was going to start her life as a trend setter with individual hand knits made from yarns that were specially selected for her!

This book contains many of Julia's designs with additions from the Harmony collection. Knits for boys have been added. We have included one or two crochet garments and a shawl which we believe are an essential part of every smart baby's wardrobe.

My daughter has just given birth to Katie. Having taught myself to knit from the Harmony Guides perhaps it is time for me to knit for Katie, just maybe......., well, maybe not!

With thanks to Julia Carpenter.

David Moeller
Publisher

General Notes

Tension
Always check your tension before starting work. If the tension piece measures **less** than the required width try a size larger needle or hook. If the piece measures **more** than the required width try a size smaller needle or hook. Where tensions are given over st st or dc for a patterned garment, check your tension in st st or dc. If you have to use a different needle or hook size a similar adjustment must be made to the all needle or hook sizes used in the pattern. A proper fit and correct size of finished garment is only possible with the correct tension.

Notes
Figures in round brackets, ( ), refer to the larger sizes. Figures or instructions in square brackets, [ ], should be repeated as stated after the brackets.

Abbreviations
Alt = alternate; **beg** = beginning; **cms** = centimetres; **ch** = chain; **ch-sp** = chain space; **dec** = decrease; **dc** = double crochet; **htr** = half treble; **inc** = increase; **ins** = inches; **k** = knit; **p** = purl; **psso** = pass slipped stitch over; **rep** = repeat; **sl** = slip; **sp** = space; **st(s)** = stitch(es); **st st** = stocking stitch (1 row knit, 1 row purl); **tbl** = through back of loop; **tog** = together; **tr** = treble; **yb** = yarn back; **yf** = yarn forward; **yfon** = yarn forward and over needle; **yo** = yarn over; **yrn** = yarn round needle.

Slip marker = make a slip knot in a short length of contrasting yarn and place on needle where indicated. On following rows slip marker from one needle to the other until pattern is established.

Yarn Equivalents		
UK	Australia	USA
3 ply	3 ply	3 ply
4 ply	4 or 5 ply	4 ply
Double knitting	8 ply	Sport yarn

The quantities of yarn stated in this book are based on average requirements and are therefore approximate.

Finishing Touches

Swiss Darning
A Swiss darned or duplicate stitch covers an individual knit stitch, giving the appearance that the design has been knitted in. Always match your tension to the knitting - too loose and the stitches will not be covered; too tight and the work will pucker.

Swiss darning horizontally
Work from right to left, thread a tapestry needle with the embroidery yarn. Bring the needle out at the base of the first stitch, take it around the top of the stitch, then insert the needle back through the base of the same stitch, thus covering the original stitch completely. For the next stitch bring needle through at the base of next stitch to the left. Continue in this way until all the appropriate stitches have been covered.

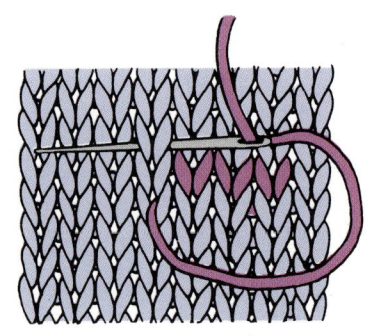

Swiss darning vertically
Work from bottom to top. Bring the needle out at the base of first stitch, then take it around top of the stitch. Insert the needle back through the base of the **same** stitch, then bring it up through the base of the stitch above, thus forming a vertical chain.

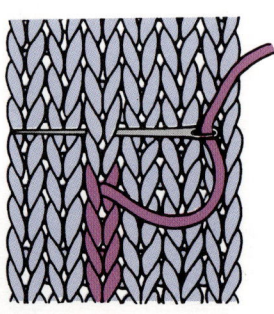

Herringbone Casing
Join waist length of elastic into a ring, making sure it is not twisted. Lay inside waistband work a herringbone stitch, from left to right over the elastic. Work into every alternate stitch, stitching just inside the top edge of the garment and just below the lower edge of the elastic. Take care not to pull the stitches tightly or catch the elastic as it must run freely within the casing.

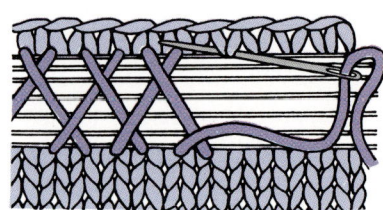

Twisted Cords
1. Cut required number of strands of yarn about three times the length of the finished cord. Four strands of yarn 100 cm [40 ins] long will produce a cord eight strands thick and approximately 35 cm [14 ins] long. Ensure the strands are equal length and knot together at each end.

2. Attach one end to a hook or door handle and insert a knitting needle through the other. Turn the knitting needle clockwise until the strands are tightly twisted. The tighter the yarns are twisted, the firmer the cord will be. They should kink up the moment the tension is released.

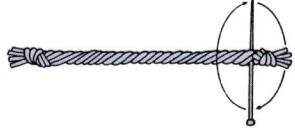

3. Holding the cord in the centre, bring ends of cord together allowing the halves to twist together. Keep the cord fairly straight to avoid tangling, smooth it out evenly. Knot cut ends together and trim. Tie a knot in folded end at the required point and cut and trim ends.

1-5
Pram Set

Measurements
To fit chest

| 40 | 45 | 50 | cm |
| 16 | 18 | 20 | ins |

Jacket
Finished Measurement

| 48 | 54 | 58 | cm |
| 19 | 21½ | 23 | ins |

Length to shoulder

| 23 | 28 | 33 | cm |
| 9 | 11 | 13 | ins |

Sleeve seam

| 13 | 15 | 17 | cm |
| 5 | 6 | 6¾ | ins |

Trousers
Inside Leg seam

| 17 | 21 | 25 | cm |
| 6¾ | 8¼ | 10 | ins |

Materials
Double Knitting Yarn

Jacket
| 150 | 150 | 200 | grams |

Trousers
| 100 | 100 | 150 | grams |

Hat, Bootees and Mitts
| 100 | 100 | 150 | grams |

Pair needles each size 4mm (8), 3¾mm (9) and 3¼mm (10). 6 toggles for Jacket. Waist length of 2 cm [¾ inch] wide elastic for Trousers.

Tension
22 sts and 30 rows = 10 cm [4 ins] square measured over st st using largest needles.

Jacket
Back
Using middle size needles cast on 53(59-64) sts and work 5 rows in garter st (every row knit).

Change to largest needles and work in st st, starting knit (first row is right side) until back measures 13(17-21) cm [5(6¾-8¼) ins] ending with a purl row. Tie a marker at each end of last row to mark start of armholes.

Next row: Knit.

Next row: K3, purl to last 3 sts, k3.

Rep the last 2 rows until back measures 10(11-12) cm [4(4¼-4¾) ins] from markers ending with a wrong side row.

Shape shoulders
Cast off 9(10-11) sts at beg of next 4 rows.

Cast off remaining 17(19-20) sts.

Left Front
Using middle size needles cast on 27(30-32) sts and work 5 rows in garter st.

Change to largest needles and continue as follows.

1st row (right side): Knit.

2nd row: K3, purl to end.

★ Rep the last 2 rows until front measures same as back to markers ending with a wrong side row. Tie a marker at side edge of last row.

Next row: Knit.

Next row: K3, purl to last 3 sts, k3.

Rep the last 2 rows until front 13(13-15) rows shorter than back to start of shoulder shaping (work 1 row more here for Right Front), thus ending at front edge.

Shape Neck
Next row: Cast off 4(5-5) sts, work to end.

Dec 1 st at neck edge on next 3 rows then following 2 alt rows. 18(20-22) sts remain. Work 5(5-7) rows straight, thus ending at side edge.

Shape Shoulder
Cast off 9(10-11) sts at beg of next row. Work 1 row. Cast off remaining 9(10-11) sts.

Right Front
Using middle size needles cast on 27(30-32) sts and work 5 rows in garter st.

Change to largest needles and continue as follows:

1st row (right side): Knit.

2nd row: Purl to last 3 sts, k3.

Complete to match Left Front from ★ to end reversing shaping by working 1 row more where indicated.

Sleeves
Using middle size needles cast on 36(38-39) sts and work 5 rows in garter st.

Change to largest needles and work 4 rows in st st, starting knit (first row is right side). Inc 1 st at each end of next and every following 6th(6th-5th) row until there are 44(48-53) sts. Work straight until sleeve measures 13(15-17) cm [5(6-6¾) ins] or required length ending with a purl row. Cast off.

Collar
Using smallest needles cast on 77(83-89) sts.

1st row (right side): K1, *p1, k1; rep from * to end.

2nd row: P1, *k1, p1; rep from * to end.

Rep the last 2 rows 4(5-6) times more.

Cast off 8(9-10) sts in rib at beg of next 6 rows.

Cast off remaining 29 sts in rib.

Pockets (Make 2)
Using largest needles cast on 18(19-20) sts and work 14(16-18) rows in st st, starting knit (right side).

Change to middle size needles and work 5 rows in garter st. Cast off knitwise.

To Finish
Read press instructions on ball band. Join shoulder seams. Fold sleeves in half lengthways and mark centre of cast off edge. Sew sleeves to side edges between markers placing centre at shoulder seams. Join side and sleeve seams. Sew shaped edge of collar to neck edge. Sew pockets to fronts as illustrated.

Using a crochet hook and 2 strands of yarn make 3 lengths of chain st each 18 cm [7 ins] long for loops. Join each chain into a ring and secure centre of loops to left front edge of boy's jacket or right front edge of girl's jacket, the first to be 9(10-12) cm [3½(4-4¾) ins] above cast on edge and placing top one 1 cm [½ inch] below start of neck shaping. Space remaining loop evenly between. Sew on toggles as illustrated.

Trousers
Left Leg
Using middle size needles cast on 39(42-45) sts and work 5 rows in garter st.

Change to largest needles and work 4 rows in st st, starting knit (first row is right side). Inc 1 st at each end of next and every following 4th row until there are 59(66-73) sts. Work straight until leg measures 17(21-25) cm [6¾(8¼-10) ins] or required length ending with a purl row.

Shape Crotch
Cast off 2 sts at beg of next 2 rows. Dec 1 st at each end of next 2(3-4) rows. 51(56-61) sts. Work straight until crotch measures 14(15-16) cm [5¼(6-6½) ins] ending with a purl row (work 1 row less here for Right Leg).

Shape Back
Next row: Work 25(28-30), turn.

Next row: Sl 1, work to end.

Next row: Work 17(19-20), turn.

Next row: Sl 1, work to end.

Next row: Work 9(10-10), turn.

Next row: Sl 1, work to end, decreasing 1 st at end of row for 2nd size only. 51(55-61) sts.

Waistband
Change to smallest needles and working across all sts continue as follows:

Next row: K1, *p1, k1; rep from * to end.

Next row: P1, *k1, p1; rep from * to end.

Rep the last 2 rows 3 times more. Cast off in rib.

Right Leg
Work as given for left leg reversing shaping by working 1 row less where indicated and 1 row more across all sts before waistband.

To Finish
Read pressing instructions on ball band. Join inside leg, front and back crotch seams. Join elastic into a ring and place inside waistband. Work a herringbone stitch over elastic onto every alt st of ribbing (see page 4), thus enclosing the elastic.

Hat
Using smallest needles cast on 61(71-81) sts.

1st row (right side): K1, *p1, k1; rep from * to end.

2nd row: P1, *k1, p1; rep from * to end.

Rep the last 2 rows twice more.

Change to largest needles and work in st st, starting knit until hat measures 11(12-13) cm [4¼(4¾-5) ins] ending with a purl row.

Shape Back
Cast off 4(4-5) sts at beg of next 8(10-10) rows.

Cast off remaining 29(31-31) sts.

Finishing and Neck Edging
Read pressing instructions on ball band. Join back seam.

Neck Edging: Using middle size needles and with right side facing pick up and k48(53-57) sts evenly around neck edge.

Work 4 rows in garter st. Cast off knitwise.

Using 2 strands of yarn make 2 twisted cords each 15 cm [6 ins] long and sew one to each corner of neck edging. Make a tassel and sew firmly to top of hat.

1-5

Bootees

Using smallest needles cast on 29(31-33) sts and knit 1 row (wrong side).

Shape Sole

1st row: K1, [inc in next st, k11(12-13) inc in next st, k1] twice. 33(35-37) sts.

2nd and every alt row: Knit.

3rd row: K2, *inc in next st, k11(12-13), inc in next st*, k3; rep from * to *, k2. 37(39-41) sts.

5th row: K3, *inc in next st, k11(12-13), inc in next st*, k5; rep from * to *, k3. 41(43-45) sts.

Continue to inc 4 sts in this way on following 1(2-3) alt rows. 45(51-57) sts.

Change to largest needles and work 7(9-11) rows in garter st (every row knit).

Shape Instep

1st row: K26(29-33), sl 1, k1, psso, turn.

2nd row: Sl 1, p7(7-9), p2tog, turn.

3rd row: Sl 1, k7(7-9), sl 1, k1, psso, turn.

Rep 2nd and 3rd rows 5(6-7) times more, then 2nd row again.

Next row: Sl 1, knit to end. 31(35-39) sts remain.

Work 5(7-9) rows in st st, starting purl.

Change to smallest needles and work 4(6-6) rows in k1, p1 rib as given for Hat. Cast off in rib.

To Finish

Join sole and back seams.

Mitts

Using smallest needles cast on 27(31-35) sts and work 4(6-6) rows in k1, p1 rib as given for Hat.

Change to largest needles and work in st st, starting knit, until mitt measures 6(7-8) cm [2½(2¾-3) ins] ending with a purl row.

Shape Top

1st row: K1, [sl 1, k1, psso, k8(10-12), k2tog, k1] twice. 23(27-31) sts remain.

2nd row: Knit.

3rd row: K1, [sl 1, k1, psso, k6(8-10), k2tog, k1] twice. 19(23-27) sts remain.

4th row: Knit.

5th row: K1, [sl 1, k1, psso, k4(6-8), k2tog, k1] twice. 15(19-23) sts remain.

6th row: Knit.

Cast off.

To Finish

Join side and top seams. Using 2 strands of yarn make a twisted cord 50(55-60) cm [20(22-24) ins] long and sew one mitt to each end.

Tassels

1. Cut a rectangle of cardboard as wide as the length of the finished tassel. Wind the yarn around the cardboard until the required thickness is reached. Break the yarn, thread it through a sewing needle and pass under all the loops. Do not remove the needle.

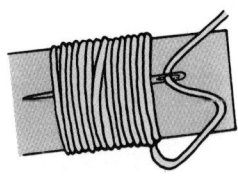

2. Tie the end of the yarn firmly around the loops, remove the card and cut through the loops at the end opposite the knot.

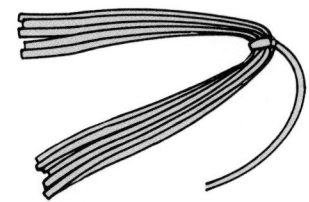

3. Wind the end of yarn around all the loops below the fold and fasten it securely. Pass the needle through the top and use to sew the tassel in place. Trim the ends neatly.

6

Baby's Blanket

Measurement

Finished Blanket measures approximately 90 x 90 cm [36 x 36 ins] including edging.

Materials

4 ply Knittting Yarn

Colour A: 150 grams, Colour B: 100 grams, Colour C: 150 grams.

Pair needles each size 3¼mm (10) and 2¾mm (12).

Tension

30 sts and 45 rows = 10 cm [4 ins] square measured over slip stitch rib pattern using larger needles.

Slip Stitch Rib Square (Make 13)

Using larger needles and A cast on 51 sts and purl 1 row. Commence pattern.

1st row (right side): Using B, k1, *yf, sl 1 purlwise, yb, k1; rep from * to end.

2nd row: Using B, purl.

3rd row: Using A, k1, *yf, sl 1 purlwise, yb, k1; rep from * to end.

4th row: Using A, purl.

These 4 rows form the pattern. Rep these 4 rows until piece measures 17 cm [6¾ ins] ending with a wrong side row. Cast off.

Diamond Pattern Square (Make 12)

Using larger needles and C cast on 47 sts.

1st row (right side): P5, *k4, p1, k4, p5; rep from * to end.

2nd row: K5, *p3, k3, p3, k5; rep from * to end.

3rd row: K7, p5, [k9, p5] twice, k7.

4th row: P6, k7, [p7, k7] twice, p6.

5th row: K5, *p9, k5; rep from * to end.

6th row: As 4th row.

7th row: As 3rd row.

8th row: As 2nd row.

These 8 rows form the pattern. Rep these 8 rows until piece measures 17

6

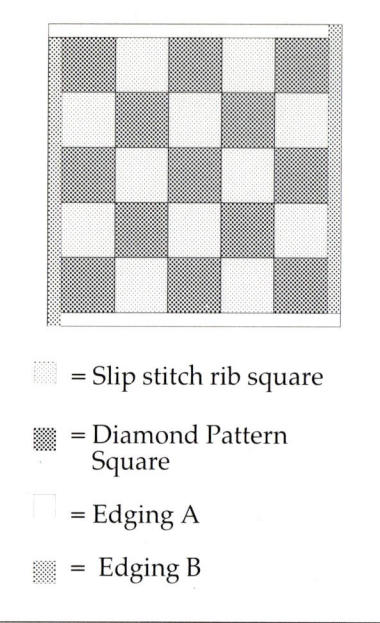

= Slip stitch rib square

= Diamond Pattern Square

= Edging A

= Edging B

Measurements

To fit chest

| 40 | 45 | 50 | cm |
| 16 | 18 | 20 | ins |

Pinafore length to shoulder

| 29 | 34 | 38 | cm |
| 11½ | 13½ | 15 | ins |

Cardigan finished measurement

| 46 | 52 | 57 | cm |
| 18½ | 21 | 23 | ins |

Length to shoulder

| 21 | 25 | 29 | cm |
| 8¼ | 10 | 11½ | ins |

Sleeve seam

| 13 | 15 | 17 | cm |
| 5 | 6 | 6¾ | ins |

Materials

Double Knitting Yarn

Pinafore

Main colour (M)

| 50 | 100 | 100 | grams |

Contrast colour A

| 50 | 50 | 50 | grams |

Contrast colour B

| 25 | 25 | 25 | grams |

Cardigan

Main colour (M)

| 50 | 50 | 100 | grams |

Contrast colour A

| 50 | 50 | 50 | grams |

Contrast colour B

| 25 | 25 | 25 | grams |

Pair needles each size 4mm (8) and 3¼mm (10). 5 buttons for cardigan.

Tension

22 sts and 30 rows = 10 cm [4 ins] square measured over st st using larger needles.

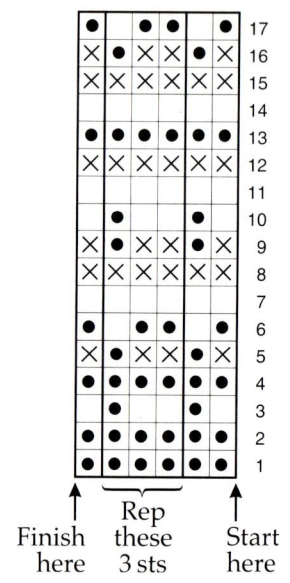

Finish here | Rep these 3 sts | Start here

☐ = Main colour (M)
● = Contrast Colour A
✕ = Contrast Colour B

Do not weave yarn in at back of work. Carry colour not in use loosely across back of work, or up side edge of work. Read every row from right to left.

cm [6¾ ins] ending with a 4th or 8th row of pattern. Cast off in pattern.

Finishing and Edging

Do not press. Join squares as shown in diagram.

Edgings

(Make 2 each in colours A and B)
Using smaller needles cast on 10 sts and work in garter st (every row knit) until piece measures 3 cm [1¼ ins] more than 1 edge of Blanket. Cast off.
Sew in place as shown in diagram.

7/8

Pinafore Dress and Cardigan

Pinafore Dress
Back

Using smaller needles and A cast on 87(101-119) sts and work 3 rows in st st starting purl (first row is wrong side).

Next row (picot): K1, *yf, k2tog; rep from * to end.

Change to larger needles and work 3 rows in st st, starting purl, increasing 1 st at end of last row for 2nd and 3rd sizes only.

Joining in M and B as required, work the 17 rows of chart. Break off A and B and continuing in M only work 7(9-11) rows in st st, starting purl.

Next row (decrease): K8(7-8), sl 1, k2tog, psso, *k14(14-17), sl 1, k2tog, psso; rep from * to last 8(7-9) sts, k8(7-9). 77(90-108) sts remain.

Work 5(7-7) rows straight.

Next row (decrease): K7(6-7), sl 1, k2tog, psso, *k12(12-15), sl 1, k2tog, psso; rep from * to last 7(6-8) sts, k7(6-8). 67(78-96) sts remain.

Work 5(7-7) rows straight.

Next row (decrease): K6(5-6), sl 1, k2tog, psso, *k10(10-13), sl 1, k2tog, psso; rep from * to last 6(5-7) sts, k6(5-7). 57(66-84) sts remain.

Continue to dec 10(12-12) sts in this way on every following 6th(8th-8th) row 1(1-2) times more. 47(54-60) sts remain.

Purl 1 row decreasing 1 st at centre for 2nd and 3rd sizes only. 47(53-59) sts remain.

Change to smaller needles and working in garter st (every row knit), work 2 rows in A, 2 rows in B and 2 rows in M.

Change to larger needles and continuing in A only work 4(6-6) rows in st st.

Shape Armholes

Cast off 4(5-6) sts at beg of next 2 rows. 39(43-47) sts remain.

Next row: K2, p2, knit to last 4 sts, p2, k2.

Next row: P2, k2, purl to last 2 sts, k2, p2 ★.

Rep the last 2 rows 8 times more.

Divide for Neck Back

★★ Next row: K2, p2, k2(3-4), p2, k2, turn and work on these 10(11-12) sts first.

Next row: P2, k2, p2(3-4), k2, p2.

Next row: K2, p2, k2(3-4), p2, k2.

Rep the last 2 rows until armhole measures 10(11-12) cm [4(4¼-4¾) ins] ending with a wrong side row. Cast off in pattern.

Slip next 19(21-23) sts at centre onto a holder. With right side facing rejoin A to neck edge of remaining 10(11-12) sts, k2, p2, k2(3-4), p2, k2. Complete to match first side.

Front

Work as given for Back to ★.

Rep the last 2 rows 4 times more.

Divide for Front Neck

Complete as given for Back from ★★ to end.

Finishing and Edgings

Read pressing instructions on ball band.

Neck Edgings: Using larger needles and A and with right side facing knit across 19(21-23) sts on holder at back neck.

Work 3 rows in st st, starting purl.

Next row: K1, *yf, k2tog; rep from * to end.

Change to smaller needles and work 3 rows in st st, starting purl. Cast off.

> **Tip**
> It is important when turning up a hem to ensure that each stitch is sewn to its own base and not to the next stitch on either side. Wrong placing will cause the hem to twist and this cannot be put right by pressing.

Work across sts of front neck in the same way.

Join side and shoulder seams. Fold picot edgings in half to inside along picot row and slip stitch loosely in place. Slip stitch side edges of neck edgings in place.

Cardigan
Back

Using smaller needles and A cast on 51(57-63) sts.

1st row (right side): K1, *p1, k1; rep from * to end.

2nd row: P1, *k1, p1; rep from * to end.

Rep the last 2 rows 4 times more.

Change to larger needles. Working in st st, starting knit and joining in M and B as required work the 17 rows of chart. Break off A and B and continue in M only until back measures 21(25-29) cm [8¼(10-11½) ins] ending with a purl row.

Shape Shoulders

Cast off 8(9-11) sts at beg of next 2 rows, then 9(10-11) sts at beg of following 2 rows. Slip remaining 17(19-19) sts onto a holder.

Left Front

Using smaller needles and A cast on 29(33-35) sts and work 9 rows in k1, p1 rib as given for Back.

Next row: Rib 6, slip these sts onto a safety pin, rib to end increasing 1 st

7/8

at end of row for 1st and 3rd sizes only. 24(27-30) sts.

★ Change to larger needles. Working in st st starting knit, work the 17 rows of chart. Break off A and B and continue in M only until front is 13(13-15) rows shorter than back to start of shoulder shaping (work 1 more row here for Right Front), thus ending at front edge.

Shape Neck
Next row: Work 2(3-3) sts, slip these sts onto a safety pin, work to end.

Dec 1 st at neck edge on next 3 rows, then following 2 alt rows. 17(19-22) sts remain. Work 5(5-7) rows straight, thus ending at side edge.

Shape Shoulder
Cast off 8(9-11) sts at beg of next row. Work 1 row. Cast off remaining 9(10-11) sts.

Right Front
Using smaller needles and A cast on 29(33-35) sts and work 4 rows in k1, p1 rib as given for Back.

Next row (buttonhole): Rib 3, yf, k2tog, rib to end.

Work 4 more rows in rib.

Next row: Inc in first st for 1st and 3rd sizes only, rib to last 6 sts, turn and slip remaining sts onto a safety pin. 24(27-30) sts.

Complete to match Left Front from ★ to end reversing shaping by working 1 row more where indicated.

Sleeves
Using smaller needles and A cast on 31(33-35) sts and work 10 rows in k1, p1 rib as given for Back increasing 2(3-4) sts evenly across last row. 33(36-39) sts.

Change to larger needles. Working in st st starting knit, work the 17 rows of chart, **at the same time** increasing 1 st at each end of 5th row then every following 6th row twice more. 39(42-45) sts.

Break off A and B and continue in M only inc 1 st at each end of every following 6th row 1(2-3) times. 41(46-51) sts. Work straight until sleeve measures 13(15-17) cm [5(6-6¾) ins] ending with a purl row. Cast off.

Finishing and Bands
Read pressing to instructions on ball band.

Left Front Band
Using smaller needles and A cast on 1 st, then with right side of left front facing, rib across sts on safety pin for front band. 7 sts.

Continue in rib until band, **when slightly stretched** fits up front edge to start of neck shaping ending with a wrong side row. Break yarn and slip sts onto a safety pin.

Sew band in place stretching evenly and mark positions for 4 buttons, the first to match existing buttonhole in right front welt and allowing for a 5th to be placed 3 rows above sts on safety pin. Space remainder evenly between.

Right Front Band
Work as given for Left Front Band but starting with wrong side of right front facing and ending with a right side row, **at the same time** making buttonholes to match markers on right side rows as before. Leave sts on needle and do not break yarn at end.

Sew band in place. Join shoulder seams.

Neckband: Continuing on from sts of right front band, knit across sts on safety pin at right front neck, pick up and k13(13-15) sts up right front slope, knit across sts on holder at back neck, pick up and k13(13-15) sts down left front slope, knit across sts on safety pin at left front neck and rib across sts of left front band. 61(65-69) sts.

Starting with a 2nd row, work 5 rows in k1, p1 rib as given for Back, making buttonhole as before on 2nd of these rows. Cast off in rib.

Fold sleeves in half lengthways and mark centre of cast off edge. Sew sleeves to side edges placing centre at shoulder seam. Join side and sleeve seams. Sew on buttons.

Tip
This versitile pattern can be equally effective if the skirt and bodice of the pinafore in the same colour.

9/10

Crochet Jacket and Bonnet

Measurements
Jacket
To fit chest sizes

| 40 | 45 | 50 | cm |
| 16 | 18 | 20 | ins |

Finished measurement at chest

| 44 | 50 | 55 | cm |
| 17½ | 20 | 22 | ins |

Length from back of neck

| 26 | 30 | 34 | cm |
| 10¼ | 11¾ | 13½ | ins |

Sleeve length

| 12 | 14 | 16 | cm |
| 4¾ | 5½ | 6 | ins |

Bonnet
Width around face

| 30 | 30 | 34 | cm |
| 12 | 12 | 13½ | ins |

Materials
Baby 4ply Knitting Yarn
Jacket

| 100 | 120 | 120 | grams |

Bonnet

| 20 | 40 | 40 | grams |

Crochet hook size 3mm. 3 buttons for Jacket. Baby ribbon for Jacket and Bonnet.

Tension
22 sts and 28 rows = 10 cms [4 ins] square measured over dc.

Special Abbreviations
Dc2tog = pull up 1 loop in each of next 2 sts, yo and through all 3 loops.
Cluster = work [2tr, 1ch, 2tr].

Jacket
Back and Fronts
(worked in one piece to armholes)

Make 140(156-172)ch.

Foundation row (right side): 1tr into 4th ch from hook (count as 2 sts), 3ch, miss next 3ch, 1dc into next ch, 3ch, *miss next 3ch, work 1 cluster into next ch (see Special Abbreviations), 3ch, miss next 3ch, 1dc into next ch, 3ch; rep from * to last 4ch, miss next 3ch, 2tr into last ch. 16(18-20) cluster plus half cluster at each end.

★**1st row:** 3ch (count as 1tr), 1tr into last tr of previous row, [3ch, 1dc into next 3ch-sp] twice, *3ch, miss next 2tr, work 1 cluster into ch-sp at centre of cluster on previous row, [3ch, 1dc into next 3ch-sp] twice; rep from * to last 2 sts, 3ch, miss next tr, 2tr into 3rd of 3ch at beg of previous row.

2nd row: 3ch (count as 1tr), 1tr into last tr of previous row, 3ch, miss next 3ch-sp, 1dc into next 3ch-sp, 3ch, *miss next 3ch-sp, work 1 cluster into ch-sp at centre of cluster on previous row, 3ch, miss next 3ch-sp, 1dc into next 3ch-sp, 3ch; rep from * to last 3ch-sp, miss 3ch-sp and tr, work 2tr into 3rd of 3ch at beg of previous row.

These 2 rows form the pattern ★. Continue in pattern until piece measures 16(18-20) cm [6¼(7-8) ins] or 2 cm [¾ inch] less than required length to armholes ending with a wrong side row.

★★**Next row:** 1ch to turn, 1dc into each of next 2tr, 1htr into next 3ch-sp, 2tr into next 3ch-sp, 1htr into next 3ch-sp, *1dc into each of next 2tr, miss next ch-sp, 1dc into each of next 2tr, 1htr into next 3ch-sp, 2tr into next 3ch-sp, 1htr into next 3ch-sp; rep from * to last 2 sts, 1dc into each of last 2 sts ★★. 136(152-168) sts.

Next row (decrease): 1ch to turn, work 1dc into each of next 2(2-3) sts, *[dc2tog] twice, 1dc into each of next 3 sts; rep from * to last 8(3-4) sts, [dc2tog] 3(1-1) times, 1dc into each st to end. 97(109-121) sts remain.

Next row (eyelets): 3ch, 1tr into each of next 2 sts, 1ch, miss next st, *1tr into next st, 1ch, miss next st; rep from * to last 3 sts, 1tr into each of next 3 sts. 46(52-58) eyelets.

Next row: 1ch to turn, work 1dc into each st to end. 97(109-121) sts.

Continuing in dc work as follows:

Divide for Raglan Armholes

Next row: 1ch to turn, work 23(26-29)dc, turn and work on these sts first for **Right Front**.

Work 1(3-3) rows straight.

Next row: 1ch to turn, work to last 3 sts, dc2tog, work 1dc. 22(25-28) sts remain.

Dec 1 st at raglan edge as before on every alt row until 18(19-19) sts remain ending with the dec row.

Shape Neck

Next row: 1ch to turn, work 1dc, dc2tog, work 12dc, turn.

Next row: 1ch to turn, dc2tog, work to last 3 sts, dc2tog, work 1dc. (1 st decreased at each end of row). 12 sts remain.

Dec 1 st at raglan edge on every row **at the same time** dec 1 st at neck edge on next 2 rows then following alt row. 5 sts remain.

Keeping neck edge straight dec 1 st at raglan edge on next 2 rows. 3 sts remain. Dec 1 st at neck edge only on following alt row. Work 1 row. Fasten off.

With right side of work facing miss next 2 sts, rejoin yarn to next st, work 1dc into same st, work 46(52-58) more dc, turn and work on these 47(53-59) sts for **Back**.

Work 1(3-3) rows straight.

Next row: 1ch to turn, work 1dc, dc2tog, work to last 3dc, dc2tog, work 1dc.

Dec 1 st at each end of every alt row as before until 37(39-39) sts remain ending with the dec row, then dec 1 st at each end of every row until 17(19-19) sts remain. Work 1 row. Fasten off.

With right side of work facing miss next 2 sts, rejoin yarn to next st, work 1 dc into same st, work in dc to end. Work on these 23(26-29) sts for **Left Front**.

Work 1(3-3) rows straight.

Next row: 1ch to turn, work 1dc, dc2tog, work to end.

Dec 1 st at raglan edge on every alt row until 18(19-19) sts remain ending with the dec row.

9/10

Shape Neck

Next row: Sl st across first 4(5-5) sts, 1ch (not counted as a st), work to last 3 sts, dc2tog, work 1dc. 14 sts remain.

Next row: 1ch to turn, work 1dc, dc2tog, work to last 2 sts, dc2tog. 12 sts remain.

Dec 1 st at raglan edge on every row **at the same time** dec 1 st at neck edge on next 2 rows then following alt row. 5 sts remain. Keeping neck edge straight dec 1 st at raglan edge on next 2 rows. 3 sts remain. Dec 1 st at neck edge only on following alt row. Work 1 row. Fasten off.

Sleeves

Make 32(34-36)ch, work 1dc into 2nd ch from hook, 1dc into each ch to end. 31(33-35)dc.

Work 2 rows in dc.

Next row (increase): 1ch to turn, work 7(2-2)dc, [work 2dc into next dc, work 14(3-5)dc] 1(7-5) times, work 2dc into next dc, work 8(2-2)dc. 33(41-41)dc.

Foundation row (right side): 3ch (count as 1tr), 1tr into first dc, 3ch, miss next 3dc, 1dc into next dc, *3ch, miss next 3dc, work 1 cluster into next dc, 3ch, miss next 3dc, 1dc into next dc; rep from * to last 4dc, 3ch, miss next 3dc, 2tr into last dc. 3(4-4) clusters plus half cluster at each end.

Work as given for Back and Fronts from ★ to ★. Continue pattern until sleeve measures 11(13-15) cm [4¼(5-5¾) ins] or 1 cm [½ inch] less than required seam length ending with a wrong side row.

Work as given for Back and Fronts from ★★ to ★★. 32(40-40) sts.

Next row (increase): 1ch to turn, work 1dc into each of next 3(2-2) sts, *work 2dc into next st, work 1dc into each of next 4 sts; rep from * to last 4(3-3) sts, work 2dc into next st, work 1dc into each st to end. 38(48-48)dc.

Shape Raglan Top

1st row: Sl st across first dc, work to last st, turn. 36(46-46) sts remain.

Work 1 row straight.

3rd row: 1ch to turn, work 1dc, dc2tog, work to last 3dc, dc2tog, work 1dc.

Rep the last 2 rows until 26(34-22) sts remain ending with the dec row,

then rep the last row only until 6 sts remain. Work 1 row. Fasten off.

Finishing and Edgings

Read pressing instructions on ball band. Join raglan and sleeve seams.

Edging: With right side of work facing join yarn to lower edge of skirt at centre back and work 1 row of firm dc all round edge of jacket working 3dc into each outer corner, sl st to join.

Next round: 3ch, 1dc into first st, miss next st, 1dc into next st, *3ch, 1dc into same st as last dc, miss next dc, 1dc into next dc; rep from * to end of round, sl st into first of 3ch at beg of round. Fasten off.

Cuffs: With right side of work facing rejoin yarn at sleeve seam and work a row of firm dc, sl st to join.

Next round: Work as given for Edging of main piece.

Mark positions on left front edge for 3 buttons, the first on neck edge and the 3rd 1 cm [½ inch] above eyelet row. Space remaining button halfway between.

Press seams. Sew on buttons using corresponding loops in edging on right front for buttonholes. Thread ribbon through eyelets as illustrated. Thread shirring elastic through cuffs if required.

Bonnet

Make 60(60-68)ch and work Foundation row as given for Back and Fronts of Jacket. 6(6-7) clusters plus half cluster at each end.

Work as given for Back and Fronts of Jacket from ★ to ★. Continue in pattern until bonnet measures 11(12-13) cm [4¼(4¾-5) ins] ending with a wrong side row. Place a marker at each end of last row. Work as given for Back and Fronts of Jacket from ★★ to ★★. 56(56-64) sts.

Next row (increase): 1ch to turn, work 1dc into each of next 3 sts, *work 2dc into next st, work 1dc into each of next 5(5-6) sts; rep from * to last 5 sts, work 2dc into next st, work 1dc into each st to end. 65(65-73)dc.

Shape Back

1st row: 1ch to turn, 1dc into next st, *dc2tog, 1dc into each of next 6 sts;

rep from * to end. 57(57-64) sts remain.

2nd and every alt row: 1ch to turn, work in dc to end.

3rd row: 1ch to turn, 1dc into next st, *dc2tog, 1dc into each of next 5 sts; rep from * to end.

49(49-55) sts remain.

5th row: 1ch to turn, 1dc into next st, *dc2tog, 1dc into each of next 4 sts; rep from * to end.

41(41-46) sts remain.

Continue to dec 8(8-9) sts in this way on every alt row until 17(17-19) sts remain ending with the wrong side row.

Next row: 1ch to turn, 1dc into next st, *dc2tog; rep from * to end.

Fasten off. Thread yarn through top of remaining 9(9-10) sts, draw up firmly and secure.

Finishing and Edging

Read pressing instructions on ball band. Join back seam to markers.

Face Edging: With right side of bonnet facing work a row of firm dc around face edge, turn.

Next row: 3ch, 1dc into first dc, *miss next dc, 1dc into next dc, 3ch, 1dc into same st as last dc; rep from * to end. Fasten off.

Neck Edging: With right side of bonnet facing work 2 rows of firm dc along neck edge. Fasten off.

Sew a length of ribbon firmly to each corner of bonnet as illustrated.

11-13

Helmet, Bootees and Mitts

Size

To fit Birth to 6 months.

Materials

Double Knitting Yarn

Helmet: 50grams Main colour (M), oddment of Contrast colour (C).

Bootees: 25grams each Main colour (M) and Contrast colour (C). **Mitts:** 20grams Main colour (M), oddment of Contrast colour (C).
Pair needles each size 4mm (8) and 3¼mm (10). 1 button for Helmet.

Tension
22 sts and 30 rows = 10 cm [4 ins] square measured over st st using larger needles.

Helmet
Right ear flap
Using smaller needles and M cast on 9 sts.

1st row (right side): K1, *p1, k1; rep from * to end.

2nd row: P1, *k1, p1; rep from * to end.

Rep the last 2 rows once more.

Next row (buttonhole): Rib 4, yrn, p2tog, rib to end.

Work 3 more rows in rib. Keeping rib correct inc 1 st at each end of next and every alt row until there are 25 sts.

Work straight until piece measures 8 cm [3 ins] ending with a 2nd row. Break yarn and slip sts onto a spare needle.

11-13

Left Ear Flap

Work as given for Right Ear Flap, omitting buttonhole.

Main Piece

Using smaller needles and M cast on 10 sts, then continuing on from these sts and with right side of work facing, rib across sts of left ear flap, turn and cast on 39 sts, turn and work in rib across sts of right ear flap, turn and cast on 10 sts. 109 sts.

Work in rib as given for Right Ear Flap starting with the 2nd row until main piece measures 10 cm [4 ins] ending with a wrong side row.

Shape Crown

1st row: Rib 8, *k3tog, rib7; rep from * to last 11 sts, k3tog, rib to end. 89 sts remain.
2nd and every alt row: P1, *k1, p1; rep from * to end.
3rd row: Rib 7, *p3tog, rib 5; rep from * to last 10 sts, p3tog, rib to end. 69 sts remain.
5th row: Rib 6, *k3tog, rib 3; rep from * to last 9 sts, k3tog, rib to end. 49 sts remain
7th row: Rib 5, *p3tog, k1; rep from * to last 8 sts, p3tog, rib to end. 29 sts remain.
9th row: K1, *k2tog; rep from * to end.
Break yarn, thread through remaining 15 sts, draw up firmly and fasten off.

Brim

Using larger needles and M cast on 64 sts thumb method. Working in garter st (every row knit - 1st row is right side), work 2 rows in C and 2 rows in M.
Rep the last 4 rows until piece measures approximately 4 cm [1½ ins] ending with the first row of M stripe. Using M cast off knitwise.

To Finish

Read pressing instructions on ball band. Join back seam of helmet. Join brim into a ring. Pin brim in place with cast on edge to lower edge of main piece. Slip stitch lower edge of brim in place. Sew on buttons. If required make a pom pom and sew firmly to top of crown.

Bootees

Using larger needles and m cast on 37 sts.
1st row (right side): [K1, inc in next st, k15, inc in next st] twice, k1.
2nd row: Knit.
3rd row: [K1, inc in next st, k17, inc in next st] twice, k1.
4th row: Knit.
5th row: [K1, inc in next st, k19, inc in next st] twice, k1. 49 sts.
Continuing in garter st (every row knit), work 3 rows in M, 2 rows in C, 2 rows in M, 2 rows in C and 1 row in M.

Shape Instep

1st row: Using M, k10, p18, p3tog, turn.
2nd row: Using M, sl 1, k7, sl 1, k2tog, psso, turn.
3rd row: Using M, sl 1, p7, p3tog, turn.
Rep 2nd and 3rd rows 3 times more, then work 2nd row once again. 29 sts remain.
Next row: Using M, knit to end.
Using C work 2 rows in garter st.
Next row (eyelets): Using M, k1, *yf, k2tog; rep from * to end.
Working in garter st work 1 row in M, 2 rows in C and 2 rows in M. Rep the last 4 rows once more, then knit 2 rows in C and 1 row in M. Using M cast off knitwise.

To Finish

Read pressing instructions on ball band. Join foot and heal seams. Using 2 strands of C make 2 twisted cords 46 cm [18 ins] long and thread through eyelet holes as illustrated.

Mitts

Using larger needles and M cast on 27 sts thumb method.
Working in garter st (every row knit - **1st row** is right side), work 2 rows in C and 2 rows in M.
Rep the last 4 rows twice more, then work the first 2 rows again. Break off C and continue in M only.
Next row (eyelets): K2, *yf, k2tog; rep from * to last st, k1.
Work in st st, starting purl, until mitt measures 6 cm [2½ ins] from eyelet row ending with a purl row.

Shape Top

1st row: K3, *k2tog, k2; rep from * to end. 21 sts remain.
2nd row: Purl.
3rd row: K3, *k2tog, k1; rep from * to end. 15 sts remain.
4th row: Purl.
5th row: K1, *k2tog; rep from * to end.
Break yarn, thread through remaining 8 sts, draw up firmly and fasten off.

To Finish

Read pressing instructions on ball band. Join seam. Using 2 strands of C make 2 twisted cords 36 cm [14 ins] long and thread through eyelet holes as illustrated.

14

Crochet Shawl

Finished Measurement

Approximately 142 cm [56 ins] square.

Materials

Baby 3ply Knitting Yarn: approximately 650 grams.
3mm crochet hook.

Tension

Motif: measures approximately 12.5 x 12.5 cm [5 x 5 ins].
Border and joining pattern: 4 patterns of [2tr, 2ch] and 8 rows = 6 cm 2½ ins] square.

Motif (Make 64)

Make 6ch, sl st into first ch to form a ring.
1st round: 3ch (count as 1tr), work 15tr into ring, sl st into 3rd of 3ch at beg of round.
2nd round: 5ch (count as 1tr, 2ch), *work 1tr into next tr, 2ch; rep from * to end, sl st into 3rd of 5ch at beg of round.
3rd round: Sl st into first 2ch sp, 3ch, 2tr into same sp as sl st, 1ch, *work

3tr into next sp, 1ch; rep from * to end, sl st into 3rd of 3ch.

4th round: *[3ch, work 1dc into next ch-sp] 3 times, 4ch, 1dc into next ch-sp; rep from * 3 times more, sl st into 1st of 3ch at beg of round.

5th round: Sl st into first arch, 3ch, work 2tr into same arch as sl st, 2tr into next arch, 3tr into next arch, work [3tr, 4ch, 3tr] into 4ch arch at corner, *3tr into next arch, 2tr into next arch, 3tr into next arch, [3tr, 4ch, 3tr] into next corner 4ch arch; rep from * twice more, sl st into 3rd of 3ch.

6th round: 3ch, work 1tr into each of next 10tr, [3tr, 1ch, 3tr] into 4ch arch at first corner, *1tr into each of next 14tr, [3tr, 1ch, 3tr] into 4ch arch at next corner; rep from * twice more, 1tr into each of next 3tr, sl st into 3rd of 3ch.

7th round: 3ch, work 1tr into each of next 13tr, [2tr, 1ch, 2tr] into corner ch-sp, *1tr into each of next 20tr, [2tr, 1ch, 2tr] into next ch-sp; rep from * twice more, 1tr into each of last 6tr, sl st into 3rd of 3ch. Fasten off.

Border and Joining Pattern
Make 294 loose ch. Work 1dc into 2nd ch from hook, 1dc into next ch, *2ch, miss 1ch, 1dc into each of next 2ch; rep from * to end, turn.
Note: Count each 2ch as **1 st only** throughout. Commence Pattern
1st row (right side): 3ch (count as 1tr), miss first dc, 1tr into next dc, *2ch, 1tr into each of next 2dc; rep from * to end, turn. 97 patterns of [2tr, 2ch] plus 2tr.

2nd row: 1ch, work 1dc into each of first 2tr, *2ch, 1dc into each of next 2tr; rep from * to end, placing last dc into 3rd of 3ch at beg of previous row, turn.
Rep the last 2 rows 5 times more, then 1st row again.

★ **Joining row**: 1ch, work [2dc, 2ch] 6 times, sl st into next tr, **take one of the motifs and, with right sides together, place motif behind border and sl st into ch-sp at corner of motif, sl st into next tr on border, *miss 1tr on motif, sl st into next tr, sl st into next tr on border, miss 1tr on motif, sl st into next tr, sl st into ch sp on border , miss 1tr on motif, sl st into next tr, miss 1tr on border, sl st into next tr; rep from * 3 times more, sl st into ch-sp at next corner of motif, then sl st back into last tr worked into on border, 2ch, [2dc, 2ch] twice, sl st into next tr; rep from ** until 8 motifs have been joined to form a row, work in pattern to end, turn.

Work Right Side Panel
1st row: 3ch, miss first dc, 1tr into next dc, 2ch, [2tr, 2ch] 5 times (6 patterns worked), miss first tr at side edge of first motif, sl st into next tr, turn.

2nd row: *2ch, 2dc; rep from * to end, turn.

3rd row: Work 6 patterns, miss next 2tr at side of motif, sl st into next tr, turn.

4th row: As 2nd row.

5th row: Work 6 patterns, miss next tr at side of motif, sl st into next tr, turn.

6th row: As 2nd row.
Rep the last 4 rows 3 times more, then 3rd and 4th rows again working sl st into ch-sp at corner of motif. Lengthen remaining loop and drop from hook. Do not break yarn and work from new ball of yarn as follows:

Work Intermediate Joining Panel
With right side facing, rejoin yarn to 2nd tr on remaining side of previous motif and work as follows:

1st row: [2ch, 2tr] twice, 2ch, miss first tr on side of next motif, sl st into next tr, turn.

2nd row: [2ch, 2dc] twice, 2ch, sl st into same tr as before on previous motif, then sl st into each of next 3tr on motif, turn.

3rd row: [2ch, 2tr] twice, 2ch, miss 2tr on side of next motif, sl st into next tr, turn.

4th row: [2ch, 2dc] twice, 2ch, sl st into same tr as before on previous motif, then sl st into each of next 2tr on motif, turn.
Rep the last 4 rows 3 times more, then 1st and 2nd rows again working sl sts into corner ch-sp of each motif. Fasten off.
Work intermediate joining panels between each pair of motifs in the same way.

Work Left Side Panel
With right side facing rejoin yarn to 2nd tr at side edge of last motif and work as follows:

1st row: [2ch, 2tr] 6 times (6 patterns worked), turn.

2nd row: 1ch, [2dc, 2ch] 6 times, sl st into same tr on last motif as before, sl st into each of next 3tr, turn.

3rd row: As 1st row.

4th row: 1ch, [2dc, 2ch] 6 times, sl st into same tr on motif as last sl st, sl st

into each of next 2tr, turn.

5th row: As 1st row.

Rep the last 4 rows 3 times more.

18th row: 1ch, [2dc, 2ch] 6 times, sl st into same tr on motif as last sl st, sl st into each of last 2tr and into ch-sp at corner, turn.

19th row: As 1st row.

20th row: 1ch, [2dc, 2ch] 6 times, sl st into corner ch-sp of motif. Fasten off.

Linking Row

With right side facing pick up dropped loop at edge of right side panel and work as follows:

Work 6 patterns, *1tr into top corner ch-sp on next motif, 1tr into first tr, **2ch, miss 1tr on motif, 1tr into each of next 2tr; rep from ** 7 times more placing last tr into 2nd top ch-sp, 2ch, [2tr, 2ch] twice across intermediate panel; rep from * 6 times more, then work along last motif as for previous motifs and [2ch, 2tr] 6 times across left side panel ★★.

Work 4 rows in pattern across full width of shawl, thus ending with a right side row ★.

Rep from ★ to ★ 6 times more, then from ★ to ★★ again.

Work 13 rows in pattern across full width of shawl, thus ending with a wrong side row, turn.

Edging

1st round (right side): 1ch, work 2dc into first dc, 1dc into next dc, *1dc into 2ch-sp, 1dc into each of next 2dc; rep from * to end working 3dc into last dc. Continue along side edge as follows: *2dc into next pattern, 3dc into next pattern; rep from * to end working 3dc into corner st, work across starting ch as follows: miss first ch, 1dc into next ch, miss 1ch, 1dc into each of next 2ch; rep from * to end working 3dc into last ch, then work along remaining side edge working 5dc into every 2 patterns as for first side edge, 1dc into same st as first 2dc at beg of round, sl st into first dc.

2nd round: 3ch, work 5tr into same dc as last sl st, *miss 2dc, 1dc into next dc, miss 2dc, **7tr into next dc, miss 2dc, 1dc into next dc, miss 2dc; rep from ** to corner dc, work 11tr into corner dc*; rep from * to * 3 times more omitting 6tr at end of last rep, sl st into 3rd of 3ch. Fasten off. Do not press.

15-17
2-Colour Pram Set

Measurements

To fit chest sizes

| 40 | 45 | 50 | cm |
| 16 | 18 | 20 | ins |

Jacket
Finished measurement

| 44 | 50 | 55 | cm |
| 17½ | 20 | 22 | ins |

Length to top of shoulder

| 27 | 30 | 34 | cm |
| 10¾ | 12 | 13½ | ins |

Sleeve seam

| 13 | 15 | 17 | cm |
| 5 | 6 | 6¾ | ins |

Materials

Double Knitting Yarn

Jacket and Hat
Main colour (M)

| 150 | 150 | 200 | grams |

Contrast colour (C)

| 50 | 50 | 50 | grams |

Leggings

| 150 | 150 | 150 | grams |

Contrast colour (C)

| 25 | 25 | 25 | grams |

Pair needles each size 4mm (8) and 3¼mm (10). Cable needle for Jacket and Hat. 4 buttons for Jacket. Waist length 2 cm [¾inch] wide elastic for Leggings.

Tension

22 sts and 30 rows = 10 cm [4 ins] square measured over st st using larger needles.

Special Abbreviations

C4B or C4F (Cable 4 Back or Cable 4 Front) = slip next 2 sts onto cable needle and hold at back (or front) of work, knit next 2 sts from left-hand needle, then knit sts from cable needle.

Jacket
Back

Using smaller needles and C cast on 65(73-81) sts.

1st row (right side): K1, *p1, k1; rep from * to end.

2nd row: P1, *k1, p1; rep from * to end.

Rep the last 2 rows twice more. Break off C.

Change to larger needles, join in M and work 6 rows in st st, starting knit. Dec 1 st at each end of next and every following 4th row until 49(55-61) sts remain. Work straight until back measures 18(19-21) cm [7(7½-8¼) ins], or required length to armholes ending with a purl row.

Shape Raglan Armholes

Cast off 3(2-1) sts at beg of next 2 rows.

3rd row: K1, sl 1, k1, psso, knit to last 3 sts, k2tog, k1.

4th row: Purl.

Rep the last 2 rows until 19(21-23) sts remain ending with the purl row.

Next row: K1, sl 1, k2tog, psso, knit to last 4 sts, k3tog, k1.

Next row: Purl.

Cast off remaining 15(17-19) sts.

Left Front

Using smaller needles and C cast on 37(41-45) sts and work 5 rows in k1, p1 rib as given for Back.

Next row: Rib 8, slip these sts onto a safety pin for front band, rib 4, inc in next st, rib to end. 30(34-38) sts.

Break off C, change to larger needles, join in M and commence pattern:-

1st row: Knit.

2nd row: P1, k2, p4, k2, purl to end.

3rd row: Knit to last 7 sts, C4B, (see Special Abbreviations), knit to end.

4th row: As 2nd row.

★These 4 rows form the pattern.

21

Keeping pattern correct work 2 more rows. Dec 1 st at **beg** (side edge) of next and every following 4th row until 22(25-28) sts remain. Work straight until front measures same as back to armholes ending with a wrong side row (work 1 row more here for Right Front).

Shape Raglan Armholes

Cast off 3(2-1) sts at beg of next row ★. Work 1 row.

3rd row: K1, sl 1, k1, psso, work to end.

4th row: Work to last 2 sts, p2.

Rep the last 2 rows until 11(13-14) sts remain ending with the dec row.

Shape Neck

Cast off 1(2-3) sts at beg of next row. Continuing to dec 1 st at raglan edge as before on next and following alt row **at the same time** dec 1 st at neck edge on next 3 rows. 5(6-6) sts remain. Keeping neck edge straight continue to dec at raglan edge as before until 3 sts remain. Dec 1 st at neck edge only on following alt row. Cast off.

Right Front

Using smaller needles and C cast on 37(41-45) sts and work 5 rows in k1, p1 rib as given for Back.

Next row: Rib to last 13 sts, inc in next st, rib to last 8 sts, turn and slip these sts onto a safety pin for front band. 30(34-38) sts.

Break off C, change to larger needles, join in M and commence pattern:-

1st row: Knit

2nd row: Purl to last 9 sts, k2, p4, k2, p1.

3rd row: K3, C4F, knit to end.

4th row: As 2nd row.

Work as given for Left Front from ★ to ★ reversing shaping by reading **end** for **beg** and working one row more where indicated.

2nd row: Work to last 3 sts, k2tog, k1.

3rd row: P2, work to end.

Rep the last 2 rows until 11(13-14) sts remain ending with the wrong side row.

Shape Neck

Next row: Cast off 1(2-3) sts, work to last 3 sts, k2tog, k1.

Dec 1 st at raglan edge as before on following alt row **at the same time** dec 1 st at neck edge on next 3 rows. 5(6-6) sts remain. Keeping neck edge straight continue to dec at raglan edge as before until 3 sts remain. Dec 1 st at neck edge only on following alt row. Cast off.

Sleeves

Using smaller needles and C cast on 31(33-35) sts and work 6 rows in k1, p1 rib as given for Back increasing 1 st at centre of last row. 32(34-36) sts. Break off C, change to larger needles, join in M and commence pattern:-

1st row: Knit.

2nd row: P12(13-14), k2, p4, k2, p12(13-14).

3rd row: K14(15-16), C4B, k14(15-16).

4th row: As 2nd row.

These 4 rows form the pattern. Continuing in pattern inc 1 st at each end of next and every following 3rd(4th-5th) row until there are 44(46-48) sts. Work straight until sleeve measures 13(15-17) cm [5(6-6¾) ins], or required seam length ending with a wrong side row.

Shape Raglan Top

Cast off 3(2-1) sts, at beg of next 2 rows.

3rd row: K1, sl 1, k1, psso, work to last 3 sts, k2tog, k1.

4th row: P2, work to last 2 sts, p2.

Rep the last 2 rows until 16(12-8) sts remain ending with the wrong side row.

1st(2nd) sizes only

Next row: K1, sl 1, k2tog, psso, work to last 4 sts, k3tog, k1.

Next row: P2, work to last 2 sts, p2.

1st size only: Rep the last 2 rows once more.

All sizes: Cast off remaining 8 sts.

Collar

Using smaller needles and C cast on 83(95-99) sts and work 4 cms [1½ ins] in k1, p1 rib as given for Back. Cast off 7(8-8) sts in rib at beg of next 8 rows. Cast off remaining 27(31-35) sts.

Finishing and Bands

Read pressing instructions on ball band.

Left Front Band: Using smaller needles and C cast on 1 st and with right side of left front facing, rib across sts on safety pin for front band. 9 sts. Continue in rib until band, **when slightly stretched,** fits up front to start of neck shaping, ending with a right side row. Cast off in rib.

Sew band in place stretching evenly and mark positions for 4 buttons, the first to be 11(12-14) cm [4¼(4¾-5½) ins] above lower edge and the 4th 1 cm [½ inch] below neck shaping. Space remaining 2 evenly between.

Right Front Band: Work as given for Left Front Band but starting with wrong side of right front facing and ending with a wrong side row, **at the same time** making buttonholes to match markers on right side rows as follows:- Rib 4, yrn, p2tog, rib to end.

Sew right front band in place. Join raglan, side and sleeve seams. Sew cast off edge of collar to neck edge, starting and finishing halfway across front bands. Press seams. Sew on buttons.

Leggings
Right Leg

Using smaller needles cast on 51(55-59) sts and work 10 rows in k1, p1 rib as given for Back of Jacket.

Change to larger needles.

Shape Back

Next row: K10, turn.

Next and every alt row: Sl 1, purl to end.

Next row: K16, turn.

Continue to work 6 sts more on every alt row until the row 'K34 turn' has been worked.

Next row: Sl 1, purl to end.

Continuing in st st work 4 rows across all sts. Inc 1 st at beg (back edge) of next and every following 8th row 6 times in all. 57(61-65) sts. Work straight until piece measures 19(20-21) cm [7½(8-8¼) ins] from beg, measured at front edge and ending with a wrong side row. Mark each end of last row with contrasting yarn.

Shape Leg

Dec 1 st at each end of next 3 rows,

15-17

then every alt row until 41(47-53) sts remain, then every following 4th row until 27(29-31) sts remain. Work straight until leg measures 17(20-23) cm [6¾(8-9) ins] from markers ending with a wrong side row.★

Shape Instep
Next row: K24(25-26) sts, turn.
Next row: P14 turn.
Work 16(20-22) rows on these 14 sts. Break yarn and rejoin to inside edge of 10(11-12) sts left on needle, then with right side facing pick up and k12(14-16) sts along side of instep, work across 14 sts on needle, pick up and k12(14-16) sts along other side of instep and work across remaining 3(4-5) sts. 51(57-63) sts. Work 9 rows in garter st (every row knit).

Shape Sole
1st row: K3, k2tog, k1, k2tog, k18(21-24), k2tog, k2, k2tog, knit to end.
2nd row: Knit.
3rd row: K2, k2tog, k1, k2tog, k16(19-22), k2tog, k2, k2tog, knit to end.
4th row: Knit.
5th row: K1, k2tog, k1, k2tog, k14(17-20), k2tog, k2, k2tog, knit to end.
Cast off.

Left Leg
Work as given for right leg to ★ reversing shaping by reading knit for purl and purl for knit.

Shape Instep
Next row: K17(18-19 sts, turn.
Next row: P14, turn.
Work 16(20-22) rows on these 14 sts. Break yarn and rejoin to inside edge of 3(4-5) sts left on needle, then with right side facing pick up and k12(14-16) sts along side of instep, work across 14 sts on needle, pick up and k12(14-16) sts along other side of instep and work across remaining 10(11-12) sts. 51(57-63) sts. Work 9 rows in garter st (every row knit).

Shape Sole
1st row: K19(22-25), k2tog, k2, k2tog, k18(21-24), k2tog, k1, k2tog, k3.
2nd row: Knit.
3rd row: K18(21-24), k2tog, k2, k2tog, k16(19-22), k2tog, k1, k2tog, k2.
4th row: Knit.
5th row: K17(20-23), k2tog, k2, k2tog, k14(17-20), k2tog, k1, k2tog, k1.
Cast off.

To Finish
Read pressing instructions on ball band. Join front, back and leg seams. Starting at centre of decrease of toe, join foot seam finishing at centre of decrease of heel, thus swinging leg seam to inside of heel. Join elastic into a ring and place inside waistband, work a herringbone st over elastic onto every alt st of ribbing, thus enclosing the elastic. Press Seams.

Hat
Ear Flaps (Make 2)
Using smaller needles and C cast on 7 sts and work 15 cm [6 ins] in k1, p1 rib as given for Back of Jacket ending with a wrong side row. Inc 1 st at each end of next and every alt row until there are 27 sts. Work 5 rows straight. Cast off.

Main Piece
Using smaller needles and C cast on 73(81-89) sts and work 4 rows in k1, p1 rib as given for Back of Jacket. Break off C. Change to larger needles, join in M and work in st st, starting knit, until piece measures

11(12-13) cm [4¼(4¾-5) ins] ending with a purl row.

Shape Crown
1st row: K7, k2tog, *k6, k2tog; rep from * to end. 64(71-78) sts remain.
2nd and every alt row: Purl.
3rd row: K6, k2tog, *k5, k2tog; rep from * to end. 55(61-67) sts remain.
5th row: K5, k2tog, *k4, k2tog; rep from * to end. 46(51-56) sts remain.
Continue to dec 9(10-11) sts on every alt row until 19(21-23) sts remain ending with a purl row.
Next row: K1, *k2tog; rep from * to end.
Break yarn, thread through remaining 10(11-12) sts, draw up firmly and fasten off.

Brim
Using larger needles and M cast on 8 sts.
1st row (right side): Knit.
2nd row: K2, p4, k2.
3rd row: K2, C4B, k2.
4th row: As 2nd row.
These 4 rows form the pattern. Continue in pattern until brim fits around hat, ending with a 4th row. Cast off.

To Finish
Read pressing instructions on ball band. Join back seam of hat. Sew on ear flaps 3(3-4) cm [1¼(1¼-1½) ins] either side of centre back seam. Join brim into a ring and slip stitch to hat above ribbing as illustrated. Press seams. Using C make a pompon and attach firmly to top of crown.

Pompons
1. Cut two circles of cardboard with a diameter slightly bigger than the size of the finished pompon. Cut a smaller hole in the centre of each circle, about half the size of the original diameter. The larger the hole, the fuller the pompon, but if it is too large the pompon will be oval. To make sure that the holes are equal and aligned, cut one in one circle, then use the opening as a template for drawing and cutting the other.

2. Holding the two circles together, wind the yarn around the ring (using several strands at a time for speed) until the ring is completely covered. As the hole in the centre gets smaller you will need to use a tapestry needle to pass the yarn through.

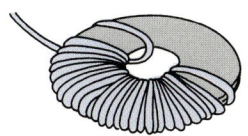

3. Cut all around the yarn at the outside edge between the two circles using a pair of sharp scissors. Make sure that all the yarn has been cut.

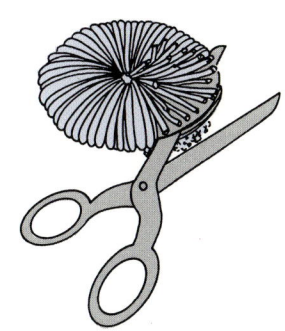

4. Separate the two circles slightly, wind a length of yarn between them and tie it **firmly** in a knot, leaving an end long enough to sew the pompon in place. Pull the two circles apart and fluff out the pompon to cover the centre join. Trim around the ends of yarn to produce a smooth shape.

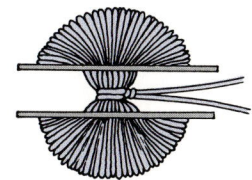

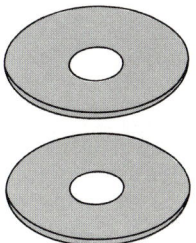

18
Slipover

Measurements
To fit chest sizes
| 45 | 50 | 55 | cm |
| 18 | 20 | 22 | ins |

Finished measurement
| 50 | 56 | 61 | cm |
| 20 | 22½ | 24½ | ins |

Length to shoulder
| 25 | 30 | 35 | cm |
| 10 | 12 | 13¾ | ins |

Materials
Double Knitting Yarn
| 100 | 100 | 100 | grams |

Pair needles each size 4mm (8) and 3¼mm (10)

Special Abbreviations
C2B (Cross 2 Back) = knit into front of 2nd st on left hand needle, then knit first st slipping both sts off needle at the same time.
C2F (Cross 2 Front) = knit into back of 2nd st on left hand needle, then knit into front of first st, slipping both sts off needle at the same time.

Tension
23 sts and 36 rows = 10 cm [4 ins] square measured over pattern using larger needles.

Back
Using smaller needles cast on 55(61-67) sts and work 4 rows in st st, starting purl.
Next row (foldline): Knit.
Change to larger needles and work 4 rows in st st, starting knit.
Next row: Purl.

Next row: Purl to end increasing 3 sts evenly. 58(64-70) sts.

Commence Pattern

1st row (right side): Knit.

2nd row: K4(3-2), p2, *k6, p2; rep from * to last 4(3-2) sts, k4(3-2).

3rd row: K3(2-1), C2B, C2F, *k4, C2B, C2F; rep from * to last 3(2-1) sts, k3(2-1).

4th row: Purl.

These 4 rows form the pattern. Continue in pattern until back measures 15(19-23) cm [6(7½-9) ins] from foldline ending with a wrong side row.

Shape Armholes

Keeping pattern correct cast off 3 sts at beg of next 2 rows. Dec 1 st at each end of next 3(3-5) rows, then following 2(3-2) alt rows. 42(46-50) sts remain★. Work straight until armholes measure 9(10-11) cm [3½(4-4¼) ins] ending with a right side row.

Shape Back Neck

Next row: Work 17(18-19) sts, turn and complete this side first.

Cast off 3 sts at beg of next and following alt row. 11(12-13) sts remain.

Shape Shoulder

Cast off 5(6-6) sts at beg of next row. Work 1 row. Cast off remaining 6(6-7) sts.

Slip next 8(10-12) sts at centre onto a holder. With wrong side facing rejoin yarn to neck edge of remaining 17(18-19) sts, cast off 3 sts, work to end. Work 1 row. Cast off 3 sts at beg of following row.

Shape Shoulder

Cast off 5(6-6) sts at beg of next row. Work 1 row. Cast off remaining 6(6-7) sts.

Front

Work as given for Back to ★.

Work straight until armholes measure 6(6-7) cm [2½(2½-2¾) ins] ending with a right side row.

Shape Neck

Next row: Work 17(18-19) sts, turn and complete this side first.

★★ Dec 1 st at neck edge on next 3 rows, then following 3 alt rows. 11(12-13) sts remain. Work straight until front measures same as back to shoulder ending at armhole edge.

Shape Shoulder

Cast off 5(6-6) sts at beg of next row. Work 1 row. Cast off remaining 6(6-7) sts.

Slip next 8(10-12) sts at centre onto a holder. With wrong side facing rejoin yarn to neck edge of remaining 17(18-19) sts and work to end.

Complete as given for first side from ★★ to end.

Finishings and Edgings

Read pressing instructions on ball band. Join left shoulder seam.

Neck Edging: Using larger needles and with right side facing, pick up and k8 sts down right back slope, knit across sts at back neck, pick up and k8 sts up left back slope and 13(14-15) sts down left front slope, knit across sts at front neck and pick up and k13(14-15) sts up right front slope. 58(64-70) sts.

★★ Work 3 rows in st st, starting purl.

Next row (foldline): Purl.

Change to smaller needles and work 3 more rows in st st, starting purl. Cast off.

Join right shoulder seam and neck edging.

Armhole edgings: Using larger needles and with right side facing, pick up and k50(54-58) sts evenly around armhole edge. Complete as given for Neck Edging from ★★ to end.

Join side seams and ends of armhole edgings. Fold lower edging, neck edging and armhole edgings to inside along foldline and slip stitch in place.

◆

19-21

Lacy Set

Size

To fit Birth to 6 months.

Materials

Baby 4ply knitting Yarn
Bonnet: 20 grams, **Bootees:** 20 grams, **Mitts:** 20 grams.

Pair of needles each size 3mm (11) and 2¾mm (12). Baby ribbon.

Tension

30 sts and 38 rows = 10 cm [4 ins] square measured over st st using larger needles.

Bonnet

Using smaller needles cast on 85 sts thumb method and work 4 rows in garter st (every row knit).

Change to larger needles and commence pattern:-

1st row (right side): P1, *k3, p1; rep from * to end.

2nd row: K1, *p3, k1; rep from * to end.

3rd row: P1, *yon, sl 1, k2tog, psso, yfrn, p1; rep from * to end.

4th row: As 2nd row.

These 4 rows form the pattern. Continue in pattern until bonnet measures approximately 11 cm [4¼ ins] ending with a 4th row of pattern. Tie a marker at each end of last row.

Shape Back

1st row: K7, sl 1, k2tog, psso, *k14, sl 1, k2tog, psso; rep from * to last 7 sts, k7. 75 sts remain.

Work 3 rows in st st, starting purl.

5th row: K6, sl 1, k2tog, psso, *k12, sl 1, k2tog, psso; rep from * to last 6 sts, k6. 65 sts remain.

6th row: Purl.

7th row: K5, sl 1, k2tog, psso, *k10, sl 1, k2tog, psso; rep from * to last 5 sts, k5. 55 sts remain.

8th row: Purl.

Continue to dec 10 sts in this way on next and every alt row until 15 sts remain.

Break yarn, thread through remaining sts, draw up firmly and fasten off.

Finishing and Edging

Read pressing instructions on ball band. Join back seam to markers.

Neck Edging: Using smaller needles and with right side of work facing pick up and k66 sts evenly round lower edge of bonnet. Work 6 rows in garter st. Cast off.

Sew a length of ribbon to each corner of bonnet.

Bootees

Using smaller needles cast on 41 sts thumb method and work 2 rows in garter st (every row knit). Change to larger needles and work 12 rows in pattern as given for Bonnet.

Next row (decrease): K2, *k2tog, k5; rep from * to last 4 sts, k2tog, k2. 35 sts remain.

Next row: Purl.

Next row (eyelets): K2, *yf, k2tog; rep from * to last st, k1. ★

Next row: Purl.

Divide for Instep

1st row: K23, turn.

2nd row: P11, turn.

Work 5 cm [2 ins] in st st on these 11 sts, ending with a purl row. Break yarn.

With right side of work facing and continuing on from the 12 sts left on right-hand needle, rejoin yarn and pick up and k15 sts evenly along side of instep, knit across the 11 sts of instep, pick up and k15 sts along other side of instep then knit across remaining 12 sts on left-hand needle. 65 sts.

Work 9 rows in st st, starting purl.

Shape Sole

1st row: K2, sl 1, k1, psso, k25, k2tog, k3, sl 1, k1, psso, k25, k2tog, k2. 61 sts remain.

2nd and every alt row: Purl.

19-21

3rd row: K2, sl 1, k1, psso, k23, k2tog, k3, sl 1, k1, psso, k23, k2tog, k2. 57 sts remain.

Continue to dec 4 sts in this way on every alt row until 49 sts remain. Cast off purlwise.

To Finish

Read pressing instructions on ball band. Join seam. Thread ribbon through eyelets as illustrated.

Mitts

Work as given for Bootees to ★.

Work in st st, starting purl, until mitt measures 6 cm [2½ ins] from eyelet row ending with a purl row.

Shape Top

1st row: K2, *sl 1, k2tog, psso, k1; rep from * to last 5 sts, sl 1, k2tog, psso, k2. 19 sts remain.

2nd row: Purl.

3rd row: K1, *k2tog; rep from * to end.

Break yarn, thread throught remaining 10 sts, draw up firmly and fasten off.

To Finish

Read pressing insructions on ball band. Join seam. Thread ribbon through eyelets as illustrated.

—◆—

22-25

4-Ply Classics

Measurements

To fit chest sizes

| 40 | 45 | 50 | 55 | cm |
| 16 | 18 | 20 | 22 | ins |

Finished measurements

| 46 | 51 | 56 | 61 | cm |
| 18½ | 20½ | 22½ | 24½ | ins |

Length from Back of Neck

| 20 | 24 | 28 | 31 | cm |
| 8 | 9½ | 11 | 12¼ | ins |

Long Sleeve Seam

| 13 | 15 | 19 | 23 | cm |
| 5 | 6 | 7½ | 9 | ins |

Short Sleeve Seam

| 4 | 4 | 5 | 5 | cm |
| 1½ | 1½ | 2 | 2 | ins |

Materials

4 Ply Knitting Yarn
Long Sleeve Sweater or Cardigan
100 100 100 100 grams
Short Sleeve Sweater or Cardigan
50 100 100 100 grams

Pair of needles each size 2¾mm (12) and 3¼mm (10). **V-Neck Sweater:** Set of 4 needles size 2¾mm (12). **Round Neck Sweater:** 2.5mm crochet hook, 3 buttons. **V-Neck Cardigan:** 4 buttons. **Round Neck Cardigan:** 5 buttons.

Tension

28 sts and 36 rows = 10 cm [4 ins] square measured over st st using larger needles.

22-25

V-Neck Sweater

Back

Using smaller needles cast on 65(71-79-85) sts.

1st row (right side): K1, *p1, k1; rep from * to end.

2nd row: P1, *k1, p1; rep from * to end.

Rep the last 2 rows 5(5-6-6) times more. Change to larger needles and work in st st, starting knit, until back measures 11(14-16-18) cm [4¼(5½-6¼-7)ins] or required length to armholes ending with a purl row.

Shape Raglan Armholes

★ Cast off 3 sts at beg of next 2 rows.

3rd row: K1, sl 1, k1, psso, knit to last 3 sts, k2tog, k1.

4th row: Purl ★.

Rep the last 2 rows until 33(35-37-39) sts remain ending with the purl row.

Next row: K1, sl 1, k2tog, psso, knit to last 4 sts, k3tog, k1.

Next row: Purl.

Rep the last 2 rows twice more. Slip remaining 21(23-25-27) sts onto a st holder for neckband.

Long Sleeves

Using smaller needles cast on 39(41-43-45) sts and work 12(12-14-14) rows in k1, p1 rib as given for Back. Change to larger needles and work 4 rows in st st, starting knit. Inc 1 st at each end of next and every following 4th(4th-5th-6th) row until there are 51(55-61-65) sts. Work straight until sleeve measures 13(15-19-23) cm [5(6-7½-9) ins] or required seam length ending with a purl row.

Shape Raglan Top

Work as given for Back from ★ to ★.

Rep the last 2 rows until 17 sts remain ending with the purl row.

Next row: K1, sl 1, k2tog, psso, knit to last 4 sts, k3tog, k1.

Next row: Purl.

Rep the last 2 rows once more. Slip remaining 9 sts onto a st holder for neckband.

Short Sleeves

Using smaller needles cast on 51(55-61-65) sts and work 8(8-10-10) rows in k1, p1 rib as given for Back.

Change to larger needles and work 6(6-8-8) rows in st st, starting knit.

Shape Raglan Top

Work as given for Shape Raglan Top of Long Sleeves.

Front

Work as given for Back to start of Raglan Shaping.

Shape Raglan Armhole and Front Neck

Next row: Cast off 3 sts, knit until there are 29(32-36-39) sts on right-hand needle after casting off, turn and complete this side first, slipping remaining sts onto a spare needle.

Next row: Purl.

Next row: K1, sl 1, k1, psso, knit to last 2 sts, k2tog.

Rep last 2 rows 4(4-3-3) times more. Continue to dec 1 st at raglan edge on every alt row as before **at the same time** dec 1 st at neck edge on every following 4th row until 7 sts remain.

Next row: Purl.

Next row: K1, sl 1, k2tog, psso, knit to end.

Rep the last 2 rows once more. 3 sts remain. Dec 1 st at neck edge only on following alt row. Cast off. Slip next st at centre front onto a safety pin. With right side of work facing rejoin yarn to neck edge of remaining sts and knit to end.

Next row: Cast off 3 sts, purl to end.

Next row: K2togtbl, knit to last 3 sts, k2tog, k1. Complete to match first side reversing shaping.

To Finish

Read pressing instructions on ball band. Join raglan seams.

Neckband: Using set of 4 needles and with right side of work facing, knit across sts on st holders at back neck and sleeve top, pick up and k29(33-39-43) sts evenly down left

22-25

front slope, knit centre front st, pick up and k29(33-39-43) sts up right front slope and knit across sts on st holder at right sleeve top.

1st round: P1, *k1, p1; rep from * to 2 sts before centre front st, sl 1, k1, psso, k1, k2tog, *p1, k1; rep from * to end.

Keeping rib correct and continuing to dec 1 st at each side of centre knit st, work 5 more rounds. Cast off in rib decreasing on this round also. Join side and sleeve seams.

Round Neck Sweater
Back and Sleeves
Work as given for Back and Sleeves of V-Neck Sweater.

Front
Work as given for Back V-Neck Sweater until 39(41-45-47) sts remain after start of raglan shaping ending with the dec row.

Shape Neck
Next row: P15(15-17-17), turn and complete this side first.

Continue to dec at raglan edge on next and every alt row **at the same time** dec 1 st at neck edge on next 3 rows, then on following 1(1-2-2) alt rows. 8 sts remain.

Next row: Purl.

Next row: K2tog, knit to last 4 sts, k3tog, k1. 5 sts remain. Purl 1 row.

Next row: K1, k3tog, k1. 3 sts remain.

Dec 1 st at neck edge only on following alt row. Cast off.

Slip next 9(11-11-13) sts at centre front onto a st holder for neckband. With wrong side of work facing rejoin yarn to neck edge of remaining sts and purl to end.

Complete to match first side reversing shaping.

To Finish
Read pressing instructions on ball band. Join front raglan seams and left back raglan seam.

Neckband: With right side of work facing and using smaller needles, knit across sts on st holder at back neck decreasing a st at centre, knit across sts at left sleeve top, pick up and k11(11-13-13) sts down left front neck, knit across sts on st holder at centre front, pick up and k11(11-13-13) sts up right front neck and knit across sts on st holder at right sleeve top.

1st row: P1, *k1, p1; rep from * to end.

Keeping rib correct work 6 more rows. Cast off in rib.

Join remaining raglan seam leaving 9 cm [3½ ins] open at top. Using crochet hook work 1 row of double crochet round opening, then work a 2nd row making 3 button loops evenly spaced on one side. Join side and sleeve seams. Sew on buttons.

V-Neck Cardigan
Back and Sleeves
Work as given for Back and Sleeves of V-Neck Sweater but casting sts off at end.

Left Front
Using smaller needles cast on 36(38-42-46) sts.

1st row (right side): *K1, p1; rep from * to last 8 sts, k8.

2nd row: K7, p1, *k1, p1; rep from * to end.

Rep the last 2 rows 5(5-6-6) times more, increasing 1 st at end of last row for 2nd and 3rd sizes only. 36(39-43-46) sts.

Change to smaller needles and keeping garter st border correct, work in st st, starting knit, until front measures same as back to armholes ending at side edge.

Shape Raglan Armhole and Front Neck
Cast off 3 sts at beg of next row.

2nd row: K7, purl to end.

3rd row: K1, sl 1, k1, psso, knit to last 9 sts, k2tog, k7.

★★ Dec 1 st at raglan edge as before on every alt row **at the same time** dec 1 st inside garter st border as before on every 4th row until 13 sts remain. ★★

Next row: K7, purl to end.

Next row: K1, sl 1, k2tog, psso, knit to end.

Rep the last 2 rows once more. 9 sts remain.

Next row: K7, p2.

Next row: Sl 1, k2tog, psso, k6.

Slip remaining 7 sts onto a safety pin.

Mark positions on garter st border for 4 buttons, the first to be on 5th row above cast on edge and the 4th to be 1 cm [½ inch] below first neck decrease. Space remaining 2 evenly between.

Right Front

Using smaller needles cast on 36(38-42-46) sts.

1st row: K8, *p1, k1; rep from * to end.

2nd row: *P1, k1; rep from * to last 8 sts, p1, k7.

Rep the last 2 rows once more.

Next row (buttonhole): K2, k2tog, yf, k4, *p1, k1; rep from * to end.

Work 7(7-9-9) more rows in rib and garter st, increasing 1 st at beg of last row for 2nd and 3rd sizes only. 36(39-43-46) sts.

Change to larger needles and keeping garter st border correct and making buttonholes to match markers on right side rows as before, work in st st, starting knit, until front measures same as back to armholes ending at side edge.

Shape Raglan Armhole and Front Neck

Cast off 3 sts at beg of next row.

Next row: K7, sl 1, k1, psso, knit to last 3 sts, k2tog, k1.

Work as given for Left Front from ★★ to ★★.

Next row: Purl to last 7 sts, k7.

Next row: Knit to last 4 sts, k3tog, k1.

Rep the last 2 rows once more. 9 sts remain.

Next row: P2, k7.

Next row: K6, k3tog.

Slip remaining 7 sts onto a safety pin.

To Finish

Read pressing instructions on ball band. Join raglan seams.

Slip sts from safety pin at top of left front onto a larger needle and work in garter st until band fits round neck to centre back. Slip sts onto a safety pin.

Work other band to match. Graft or cast sts off together and sew in place.

Join side and sleeve seams.

Sew on buttons.

Round Neck Cardigan
Back and Sleeves

Work as given for Back and Sleeves of V-Neck Sweater.

Left Front

Work as given for Left Front of V-Neck Cardigan to start of raglan and neck shaping.

Shape Raglan Armhole

Cast off 3 sts at beg of next row.

2nd row: K7, purl to end.

3rd row: K1, sl 1, k1, psso, knit to end.

Rep the last 2 rows until 23(24-26-27) sts remain ending with the dec row.

Shape Neck

Next row: Work 8(9-9-10) sts, slip these sts onto a safety pin, purl to end.

★★★ Continue to dec at raglan edge on next and every alt row as before

at the same time dec 1 st at neck edge on next 3 rows, then on following 1(1-2-2) alt rows. 8 sts remain.

Next row: Purl.

Next row: K1, sl 1, k2tog, psso, knit to last 2 sts, k2tog.

Next row: Purl.

Next row: K1, sl 1, k2tog, psso, k1. 3 sts remain.

Dec 1 st at neck edge only on following alt row.

Cast off.

Mark positions on garter st border for 4 buttons, the first on 5th row above cast on edge and allowing for a 5th to be worked on 3rd row of neckband. Space remainimg 3 evenly between.

Right Front

Work as given for Right Front of V-Neck Cardigan to start of raglan and neck shaping.

Shape Rgalan Armhole

Cast off 3 sts at beg of next row.

Next row: Knit to last 3 sts, k2tog, k1.

Next row: Purl to last 7 sts, k7.

Rep the last 2 rows until 23(24-26-27) sts remain ending with the dec row.

Shape Neck

Next row: Purl to last 8(9-9-10) sts, turn and slip remaining sts onto a safety pin.

Complete to match Left Front from ★★★ to end reversing shaping.

To Finish

Read pressing instructions on ball band. Join raglan seams.

Neckband: Slip sts from right front neck onto a smaller needle and with right side of work facing pick up and k11(11-13-13) sts up right front slope, knit across sts on st holders at right sleeve top, back neck and left sleeve top, pick up and k11(11-13-13) sts down left front slope and knit across sts on st holder at left front neck.

Next row: K7, *p1, k1; rep from * to last 8 sts, p1, k7.

Work 6 more rows in garter st and rib making buttonhole as before on the first of these rows.

Cast off in garter st and rib.

Join side and sleeve seams. Sew on buttons.

26
Playsuit

Measurements

To fit chest sizes

| 40 | 45 | 50 | cm |
| 16 | 18 | 20 | ins |

Finished measurement at chest

| 45 | 50 | 56 | cm |
| 18 | 20 | 22½ | ins |

Inside leg seam

| 15 | 17 | 19 | cm |
| 6 | 6¾ | 7½ | ins |

Length from crutch to shoulder

| 32 | 37 | 42 | cm |
| 12½ | 14½ | 16½ | ins |

Sleeve seam

| 13 | 15 | 17 | cm |
| 5 | 6 | 6¾ | ins |

Materials

Double Knitting Yarn

Colour A
| 100 | 150 | 150 | grams |

Colour B
| 50 | 50 | 100 | grams |

Colour C
| 50 | 50 | 100 | grams |

Pair needles each size 4mm (8) and 3¼mm (10). 6(6-7) buttons.

Tension

22 sts and 30 rows = 10 cm [4 ins] square measured over st st using larger needles.

Left Leg

Using smaller needles and C cast on 43(47-53) sts.

1st row (right side): K1, *p1, k1; rep from * to end.

2nd row: P1, *k1, p1; rep from * to end.

Rep the last 2 rows 3 more times then the 1st row again.

Next row (increase): Rib 1(3-1), *inc in next st, rib 3(3-4); rep from * to last 2(4-2) sts, inc in next st, rib to end. 54(58-64) sts. Break off C.

Change to larger needles and A and work 4 rows in st st, starting knit. Inc 1 st at each end of next and every following 5th(5th-6th) row until there are 64(70-76) sts. Work straight until leg measures 15(17-19) cm [6(6¾-7½) ins], or required seam length ending with a purl row.

Shape Crutch

Cast off 2 sts at beg of next 2 rows. Dec 1 st at each end of next 3 rows, then every alt row until 50(56-62) sts remain, ending with the purl row. Break yarn and slip sts onto a holder.

Right Leg

Work as given for Left Leg but leave sts on needle and do not break yarn at end.

Body

Next row: Knit to last st, then with right side of left leg facing knit together first st of left leg with last st of right leg, then knit across remaining sts of left leg. 99(111-123) sts.

Work straight until crutch measures 6 cm [2½ ins], measured straight and ending with a purl row. Tie a marker at each end of last row.

Cast off 3 sts at beg of next 2 rows. 93(105-117) sts remain. Work straight until body measures 22(26-30) cm [8¾(10¼-11¾) ins] or 2 cm [¾ inch] less than required length to armholes, measured straight from start of crutch shaping and ending with a purl row.

Break off A.

Commence Fairisle Pattern

1st row: Using C knit to end.

2nd row: Purl 1C, 1A, 1C *3A, 1C, 1A, 1C; rep from * to end.

3rd row: Knit 1A, 1C, *5A, 1C; rep from * to last st, k1A.

4th row: As 2nd row.

Break off A.

5th row: Using C knit to end.

26

27/28

Crochet Slipover and Waistcoat

Measurements

To fit chest sizes

| 45 | 50 | 55 | cm |
| 18 | 20 | 22 | ins |

Finished measurement

| 50 | 58 | 63 | cm |
| 20 | 23 | 25 | ins |

Length to shoulder (approximately)

| 25 | 30 | 34 | cm |
| 10 | 12 | 13½ | ins |

Materials

4 ply Knitting Yarn

| 50 | 100 | 100 | grams |

Crochet hook size 3.50mm.
6 buttons for waistcoat.

Special Abbreviations

1 group = into next 3ch-arch, work [1tr, 1ch, 1tr, 1ch, 1tr].

Tr2tog (treble 2 together) = work 1tr into next st until 2 loops remain on hook, 1tr into next st (or st indicated) until 3 loops remain on hook, yo and through all 3 loops.

Tension

5 pattern repeats (30 sts) and 16 rows = 11 cm [4½ ins] square measured over pattern.

Slipover

Make 68(80-86)ch, work 1dc into 2nd ch from hook, 1dc into next ch, *3ch, miss 3ch, 1dc into each of next 3ch; rep from * to last 5ch, 3ch, miss

---

Break off C. Using B purl 1 row.

Divide for Armholes

Next row: K20(23-26) sts, cast off next 4 sts, work until there are 45(51-57) sts on right-hand needle after casting off, cast off next 4 sts, work to end.

Next row: P20(23-26) sts, turn and work on these sts for **Left Front**.

Dec 1 st at armhole edge on next 3(3-5) rows, then every alt row 1(3-3) times, 16(17-18) sts remain. Work 6(6-4) rows straight thus ending at front edge.

Shape Neck

1st row: Cast off 2(3-3), purl to end.

★ Keeping armhole edge straight dec 1 st at neck edge on next 3 rows, then on following alt row once. 10(10-11) sts remain. Work 5(5-7) rows straight thus ending at armhole edge.

Shape Shoulder

Cast off 5(5-6) sts at beg of next row. Work 1 row. Cast off remaining 5 sts.

With wrong side of work facing rejoin B to next st and p45(51-57), turn and work on these sts for **Back**.

Dec 1 st at each end of next 3(3-5) rows, then every alt row until 37(39-41) sts remain. Work 17 rows straight thus ending with a purl row.

Shape Shoulders

Cast off 5(5-6) sts at beg of next 2 rows, then 5 sts at beg of following 2 rows.

Cast off remaining 17(19-19) sts.

With wrong side of work facing rejoin B to next st and purl to end. Work on these 20(23-26) sts for **Right Front.**

Dec 1 st at armhole edge on next 3(3-5) rows, then every alt row until 16(17-18) sts remain. Work 7(7-5) rows straight thus ending at front edge.

Shape Neck

1st row: Cast off 2(3-3), knit to end. Complete as given for Left Front from ★ to end.

Sleeves

Using smaller needles and C cast on 31(33-35) sts and work 10 rows in k1, p1 rib as given for Left Leg.

Change to larger needles and B and work 4 rows in st st, starting knit. Inc 1 st at each end of next and every following 5th(7th-9th) row until there are 39(41-43) sts. Work straight until sleeve measures 13(15-17) cms [5(6-6¾) ins], or required seam length ending with a purl row.

Shape Top

Cast off 2 sts at beg of next 2 rows. Dec 1 st at each end of next 3 rows, then every alt row until 25 sts remain. Dec 1 st at each end of next 3 rows. Cast off 4 sts at beg of next 2 rows. Cast off remaining 11 sts.

Collar

Using larger needles and C cast on 67(71-75) sts and work 7 rows in k1, p1 rib as given for Left Leg. Change to smaller needles and work 3 more rows in rib, keeping rib correct cast off 6(6-7) sts at beg of next 6 rows, then 7(8,7) sts at beg of following 2 rows. Cast off remaining 17(19-19) sts

Finishing and Bands

Read pressing instructions on ball band. Join shoulder seams. Join inside leg and crutch seam to markers.

Button Band: Using smaller needles and C cast on 7 sts and work in k1, p1 rib as given for Left Leg until band, **when slightly stretched** fits up front from top of crutch seam to start of neck shaping ending with a wrong side row. Cast off in rib.

Sew band to left front edge, stretching evenly. Mark position for 6(6-7) buttons, the first to be 2 cm [¾ inch] above cast on edge and the top one to be 1 cm [½ inch] below cast off edge. Space remainder evenly between.

Buttonhole Band: Work as given for Button Band but ending with a right side row, **at the same time** making buttonholes to match markers on right side rows as follows:- Rib 3, yf, k2tog, rib 2.

Sew buttonhole band to right front edge. Sew cast on edge of bands in place. Join leg and sleeve seams. Insert sleeves. Sew cast off edge of collar to neck edge starting and finishing halfway across front bands. Sew on buttons.

27/28

3ch, 1dc into each of last 2ch. 67(79-85) sts.

Commence Pattern

1st row (right side): 3ch (count as 1tr), *work 1 group into 3ch-arch, miss 1dc, 1tr into next dc; rep from * to end.

2nd row: 1ch, 1dc into first tr, 1ch, miss 1tr, 1dc into each of next ch-sp, tr and ch-sp, *3ch, miss 3tr, 1dc into each of next ch-sp, tr and ch-sp; rep from * to last 2tr, 1ch, miss 1tr, 1dc into 3rd of 3ch at beg of previous row.

3rd row: 4ch (count as 1tr, 1ch), 1tr into first ch-sp, miss 1dc, 1tr into next dc, *work 1 group into 3ch-arch, miss 1dc, 1tr into next dc; rep from * to last ch-sp, 1tr into last ch-sp, 1ch, 1tr into last dc.

4th row: 1ch, 1dc into first tr, 1dc into next ch-sp, *3ch, miss 3tr, 1dc into each of next ch-sp, tr and ch-sp; rep from * to last 5 sts, 3ch, miss 3tr, 1dc into each of 4th and 3rd of 4ch at beg of previous row.

These 4 rows form the pattern. Continue in pattern until back measures approximately 15(19-21) cm [6(7½-8¼) ins] ending with a 2nd row of pattern.

Shape Armholes

1st row: Sl st across first 4 sts, 3ch, work (1tr, 1ch, 1tr) into next 3ch-arch, miss 1dc, 1tr into next dc, work in pattern to last 3ch-arch, work 1tr into 3ch-arch, 1ch, tr2tog working first leg into same 3ch-arch, miss 1dc, work 2nd leg into next dc, turn.

2nd row: 1ch, 1dc into each of first 2 sts, 3ch, miss next 3tr, work in pattern to last ch-sp, 1dc into ch-sps, 1dc into next tr, turn.

3rd row: 3ch, work (1tr, 1ch, 1tr) into next 3ch-arch, miss 1dc, 1tr into next dc, work in pattern to last 3ch-arch, work 1tr into 3ch-arch, 1ch, tr2tog working first leg into same 3ch-arch, miss 1dc, work 2nd leg into last dc, turn.

4th row: As 2nd row.

2nd and 3rd sizes only: Rep the last 2 rows once more.

All sizes: 49(55-61) sts remain.

Next row: 3ch, *work 1 group into next 3ch-arch, miss 1dc, 1tr into next dc; rep from * to end ★.

Work 10(10-12) more rows in pattern. Fasten off.

Front

Work as given for Back to ★. Work 3(3-5) more rows in pattern.

Shape Neck

★★ **1st size only**

1st row: 3ch, [work 1 group into next 3ch-arch, miss 1dc, 1tr into next dc] twice, work 1tr into next 3ch-arch, 1ch, tr2tog working first leg into same arch, miss 1dc, work 2nd leg into next dc, turn.

2nd row: 1ch, 1dc into each of first 2 sts, 3ch, work to end.

3rd row: Work to last 3ch-arch, 1tr into 3ch-arch, 1ch, tr2tog working first leg into same arch and 2nd leg into last dc.

Rep 2nd and 3rd rows once more, then 2nd row again.

7th row: 4ch, 1tr into first ch-sp, miss 1dc, 1tr into next dc, work 1 group into 3ch-arch, 1tr into last dc. Fasten off ★★.

Miss next 2 3ch-arches and 1dc at centre, rejoin yarn to next dc, 3ch, work (1tr, 1ch, 1tr) into next 3ch-arch, miss 1dc, 1tr into next dc, work to end.

★★★ **2nd row**: Work to last ch-sp, 1dc into ch-sp, 1dc into next tr, turn.

3rd Row: 3ch, work (1tr, 1ch, 1tr) into next 3ch-arch, miss 1dc, 1tr into next dc, work to end.

Rep 2nd and 3rd rows once more, then 2nd row again.

7th row: 3ch, work 1 group into next 3ch-arch, work to end. Fasten off ★★★.

★★ **2nd size only**

1st row: 3ch, *work 1 group into next 3ch-arch, miss 1dc, 1tr into next dc; rep from * twice more but ending with tr2tog placing 2nd leg into next 3ch-arch, turn.

2nd row: 1ch, 1dc into first st, 1ch, miss 1tr, 1dc into each of next ch-sp, tr and ch-sp, work in pattern to end.

3rd row: Work to last 4dc, miss 1dc, tr2tog placing first leg into next dc and 2nd leg into last dc, turn.

Rep 2nd and 3rd rows once more, then 2nd row again.

7th row: 4ch, 1tr into next ch-sp, miss 1dc, 1tr into next dc, work 1 group into next 3ch-arch, miss 1dc, 1tr into next dc, 1tr into last ch-sp, 1ch, 1tr into last dc. Fasten off ★★.

Miss next 3ch-arch at centre, rejoin yarn to next 3ch-arch, 3ch, miss 1dc, 1tr into next dc, 1 group into next 3ch-arch, work to end.

★★★ **2nd row**: Work to last group, 1dc into each of ch-sp, tr and ch-sp of group, 1ch, miss 1tr, 1dc into next tr, turn.

3rd row: 3ch, miss next ch-sp and dc, 1tr into next dc, 1 group into next 3ch-arch, work to end.

Rep 2nd and 3rd rows once more, then 2nd row again.

7th row: 4ch, 1tr into next ch-sp, miss 1dc, 1tr into next dc, 1 group into 3ch-arch, miss 1dc, 1tr into next dc, 1tr into next ch-sp, 1ch, 1tr into last dc. Fasten off ★★★.

★★ **3rd size only**

1st row: 4ch, 1tr into ch-sp, *miss 1dc, 1tr into next dc 1 group into 3ch-arch; rep from * twice more, miss 1dc, tr2tog placing first leg into next dc and 2nd leg into 3ch-arch, turn.

2nd row: 1ch, 1dc into first st, 1ch, miss 1tr, 1dc into each of next ch-sp, tr and ch-sp, work in pattern to end.

3rd row: Work in pattern to last 4dc, miss 1dc, tr2tog placing first leg into next dc and 2nd leg into last dc, turn.

Rep 2nd and 3rd rows once more, then 2nd row again.

7th row: 3ch, [1 group into 3ch-arch, miss 1dc, 1tr into next dc] twice, 1tr into next ch-sp, 1ch, 1tr into last dc. Fasten off ★★.

Miss next 3ch-arch at centre, rejoin yarn to next 3ch-arch, 3ch, miss 1dc, 1tr into next dc, 1 group into next 3ch-arch, work in pattern to end.

★★★ **2nd row**: Work to last group, 1dc into each of ch-sp, tr and ch-sp of group, 1ch, miss 1tr, 1dc into next tr, turn.

3rd row: 3ch, miss next ch-sp and dc, 1tr into next dc, 1 group into next 3ch-arch, work to end.

Rep 2nd and 3rd rows once more, then 2nd row again.

7th row: 4ch, 1tr into ch-sp, [miss 1dc, 1tr into next dc, 1 group into 3ch-arch] twice, miss 1dc, 1tr into last dc. Fasten off ★★★.

Finishing and Edgings

Read pressing instructions on ball band. Join side and shoulder seams.

Lower Edging

With right side facing work 1 round

of firm dc (approximately 11dc to 5cm [2 ins]) evenly around lower edge of back and front, sl st into first dc.

Work 1 more round in dc, sl st into first dc.

Next round (picots): 1dc into first dc, *3ch, miss 2dc, 1dc into next dc; rep from * to end, sl st into first dc. Fasten off.

Neck and Armhole Edgings

Work around neck and armhole edges as given for Lower Edging.

Waistcoat
Back
Work as given for Back of Slipover.

Left Front

Make 32(38-44)ch, work 1dc into 2nd ch from hook, 1dc into next ch, 3ch, miss 3ch, *1dc into each of next 3ch, 3ch, miss 3ch; rep from * to last 2ch, 1dc into each of last 2ch. 31(37-43) sts.

Work in pattern as given for Back of Slipover until front measures same as back to armholes ending with a 2nd row of pattern.

Shape Armhole

1st row: Sl st across first 4 sts, 3ch, work (1tr, 1ch, 1tr) into next 3ch-arch, miss 1dc, 1tr into next tr, work in pattern to end.

2nd row: Work in pattern to last ch-sp, 1dc into ch-sp, 1dc into next tr, turn.

3rd row: 3ch, work (1tr, 1ch, 1tr) into next 3ch-arch, miss 1dc, 1tr into next tr, work to end.

4th row: As 2nd row.

2nd and 3rd sizes only: Rep the last 2 rows once more.

All sizes: 22(25-31) sts remain.

Next row: 3ch, *work 1 group into next 3ch-arch, miss 1dc, 1tr into next dc, work to end.

Work 3(3-5) more rows in pattern.

Shape Neck

Work as given for front of slipover from ★★ to ★★ following size required.

Right Front

Make 32(38-44)ch, work 1dc into 2nd ch from hook, 1dc into next ch, 3ch, miss 3ch, *1dc into each of next 3ch, 3ch, miss 3ch; rep from * to last 2ch, 1dc into each of last 2ch. 31(37-43) sts.

Work in pattern as given for Back of Slipover until front measures same as Back to armholes ending with a 2nd row of pattern.

Shape Armhole

1st row: Work in pattern to last 3ch-arch, work 1tr into 3ch-arch, 1ch, tr2tog working front leg into same arch, miss 1dc, work 2nd leg into next dc, turn.

2nd row: 1ch, 1dc into each of first 2sts, 3ch, miss next 3tr, work to end. Rep the last 2 rows 1(2-2) times more. 22(25-31) sts remain.

Next row: Work to last 3ch-arch, 1 group into 3ch-arch, 1tr into last dc. Work 3(3-5) more rows in pattern.

Shape Neck
1st size only

1st row: Sl st across first 4 sts, 3ch, work (1tr, 1ch, 1tr) into next 3ch-arch, miss 1dc, 1tr into next dc, work to end.

2nd and 3rd sizes only

1st row: Sl st across first (4-7) sts, 3ch, miss 1dc, 1tr into next dc, 1 group into next 3ch-arch work to end.

All sizes: Work as given for Front of Slipover from ★★★ to ★★★ following size required.

Finishing and Edgings

Read pressing instructions on ball band. Join side and shoulder seams.

Front Edgings

With right side facing and starting at right side seam work 1 row of firm dc (approximately 11dc to 5 cm [2 ins]) evenly along lower edge of right front, work 3dc into corner, work in dc up right front edge, work 3dc into corner at start of neck shaping, work in dc around right front neck across back neck and round left

41

front neck, work 3dc into corner at start of left front neck shaping, work in dc down left front edge, work 3dc into corner, then work in dc across lower edge of left front and back, sl st into first dc.

Work 1 more round in dc working 3dc into each corner st as before, sl st into first dc.

Next round (picots): 1dc into first dc, *3ch, miss 2dc, 1dc into next dc; rep from * to end, working 3dc into each corner st as before, sl st into first dc. Fasten off.

Armhole Edgings: With right side facing work 1 round of firm dc evenly around armhole edge, sl st into first dc.

Work 1 more round in dc, sl st into first dc.

Next round (picots): 1dc into first dc, *3ch, miss 2dc, 1dc into next dc; rep from * to end, sl st into first dc. Fasten off.

Sew 6 buttons evenly spaced to Left Front Edge. Use 3ch-picots of right front edging as button loops.

◆

29/30

Sweater and Dungarees

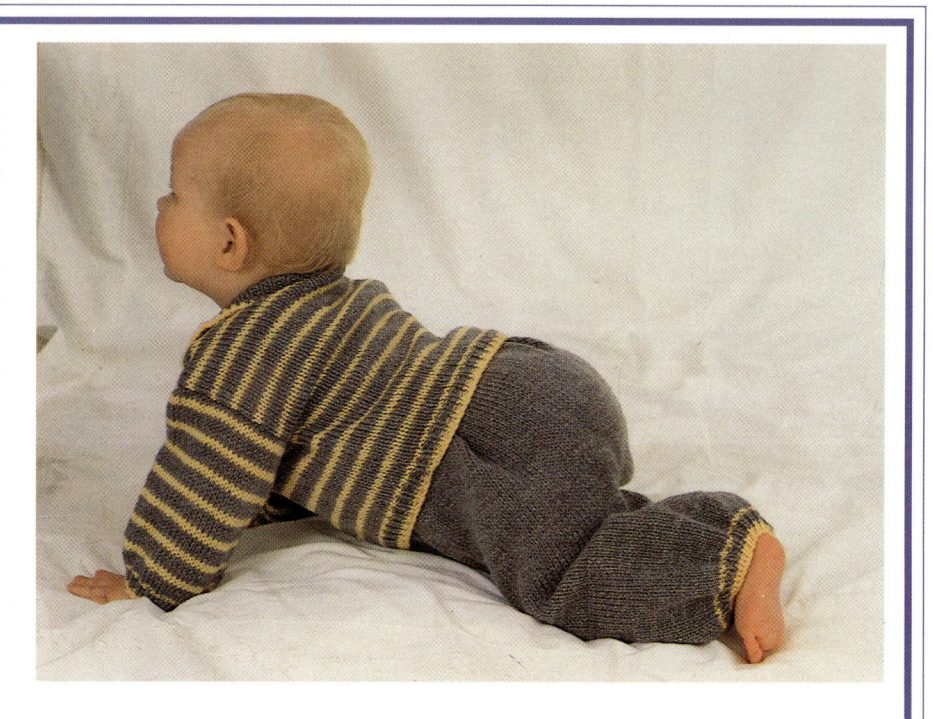

Measurements

To fit chest sizes

| 40 | 45 | 50 | 55 | cm |
| 16 | 18 | 20 | 22 | ins |

Sweater
Finished measurement

| 43 | 48 | 53 | 58 | cm |
| 17¼ | 19¼ | 21¼ | 23¼ | ins |

Length to shoulder

| 23 | 25 | 28 | 30 | cm |
| 9 | 10 | 11 | 11¾ | ins |

Sleeve length

| 15 | 17 | 18 | 19 | cm |
| 6 | 6¾ | 7 | 7½ | ins |

Dungarees
Length from shoulder to crutch

| 34 | 36 | 37 | 38 | cm |
| 13½ | 14¼ | 14½ | 15 | ins |

Leg length

| 19 | 20 | 22 | 23 | cm |
| 7½ | 8 | 8¾ | 9 | ins |

Materials

Double Knitting Yarn

Sweater
Main colour (M)

| 50 | 100 | 100 | 100 | grams |

Contrast colour (C)

| 50 | 50 | 50 | 100 | grams |

Dungarees
Main colour (M)

| 100 | 150 | 150 | 200 | grams |

Contrast colour (C)

| 50 | 50 | 50 | 50 | grams |

Pair needles each size 4mm (8) and 3¼mm (10). Circular knitting needle size 3¼mm (10), 60 cm [24 ins] long. 6 buttons.

Tension

22 sts and 30 rows = 10 cm [4 ins] square over st st using larger needles.

Special Abbreviation

M1 (Make 1 stitch) = pick up loop lying between last st worked and next st and work into back of it.

Sweater

Back

Using smaller needles and C cast on 47(53-57-63) sts.

1st row (right side): K1, *p1, k1; rep from * to end.

2nd row: P1, *k1, p1; rep from * to end.

Continuing in rib work 4 rows in M then 2 rows in C. Change to larger needles and working in st st, starting knit, work 4 rows in M and 2 in C. Rep the last 6 rows until back measures 23(25-28-30) cm [9(10-11-12) ins] ending with a purl row.

Shape Shoulders

Cast off 14(16-18-20) sts, knit until there are 19(21-21-23) sts on right-hand needle, cast off remaining 14(16-18-20) sts. Leave remaining sts on a thread.

Front

Work as given for Back until front measures 13(15-18-20) cm [5(6-7-8) ins] ending with a knit row.

29/30

Divide for Neck

Next row: P21(24-26-29), cast off next 5 sts, purl to end.

Continue on these 21(24-26-29) sts first.

★Work straight until front measures 18(20-23-25) cm [7(8-9-10) ins] ending with a knit row (work 1 row more here for 2nd side).

Shape Neck

Next row: Cast off 2(3-3-4) sts, work to end.

Dec 1 st at neck edge on next 5 rows. 14(16-18-20) sts remain. Work straight until front measures same as Back ending with a purl row. Cast off.

With right side facing, rejoin yarn to remaining 21(24-26-29) sts and knit to end. Complete as given for first side from ★ to end, working 1 row more where indicated.

Sleeves

Using smaller needles and C cast on 25(27-29-31) sts. Work first 7 rows of rib as given for Back.

Next row: Using C p3(2-2-1), *M1, p1; rep from * to last 3(2-2-1) sts, M1, purl to end. 45(51-55-61) sts.

Change to larger needles and working in st st, starting knit, work 4 rows in M and 2 rows in C. Rep the last 6 rows until sleeve measures 15(17-18-19) cm [6(6¾-7-7½) ins], or required length ending with a purl row. Cast off.

Finishing and Bands

Read pressing instructions on ball band.

Right Front Band: With right side facing, using smaller needles and C, pick up and k13 sts evenly along right front edge. Commencing with a 2nd row of rib work 1 row. Using M work 1 row.

Next row: Rib 3, cast off 1 st, rib until there are 5 sts on right-hand needle after casting off, cast off 1 st, rib to end.

Work 3 rows in rib casting on 1 st over each buttonhole on first of these rows. Using C work 1 row. Cast off in rib.

Left Front Band: Work to match Right Front Band omitting buttonholes.

Collar: Join shoulder seams. With right side facing using smaller needles and C, and starting halfway across right front band, pick up and k24(25-25-26) sts up right side of neck, work across sts at back neck as follows: k2(3-3-4), M1, [k3, M1] 5 times, k2(3-3-4), and pick up and k24(25-25-26) sts down left side of neck and across half of left front band. 73(77-77-81) sts.

Work 1 row in rib. Using M and continuing in rib work 13 rows. Using C work 1 row. Cast off in rib.

Fold sleeves in half lengthways and mark centre of cast off edge. Sew sleeves to side edge placing centre at shoulder seam. Note: armoles should measure approximately 10(12-13-14) cm [4(4¾-5¼-5½) ins]. Join side and sleeve seams. Sew edges of front bands in place. Sew on buttons.

Dungarees
Front

First Leg: Using smaller needles and C cast on 21(23-25-27) sts. Work first 7 rows of rib as given for Back of Sweater.

Next row: Using C p1(2-2-1), *M1, p1; rep from * to last 2 sts, M1, p2. 40(43-47-52) sts.

Change to larger needles and M and work in st st, starting knit, until leg measures 19(20-22-23) cm [8½(8-8¾-9) ins] or required length ending

29/30

with a purl row. Leave these sts on a thread.

2nd Leg: Work to match First Leg but leave sts on needle and do not break yarn.

Next row: Knit across sts of 2nd Leg then knit across sts of First Leg. 80(86-94-104) sts.

Continue in st st until work measures 39(41-42-43) cm [15½(16¼-16½-17) ins] ending with a knit row.

Decrease for Bib

Next row: P0(0-1-0), p2tog, [p1, p2tog] 26(28-30-34) times, p0(0-1-0). 53(57-63-69) sts remain.

Change to smaller needles and working in k1, p1 rib as given for Back of Sweater, work 2 rows in C and 4 rows in M. Rep the last 6 rows until bib measures 6(8-9-10) cm ending with a wrong side row.

Divide for Straps

Next row: Rib 13(15-17-19) sts, turn. ★Keeping pattern correct throughout work straight on these sts until bib measures 14(15-17-18) cm [5½(6-6¾-7) ins] ending with a wrong side row.

Next row: Rib 4 sts, cast off 1 st, rib until there are 3(5-7-9) sts on right-hand needle after casting off, cast off 1 st, rib to end.

Work 3 more rows casting on 1 st over each buttonhole on first of these rows. Cast off in rib.

With right side facing rejoin yarn to remaining sts, cast off next 27(27-29-31) sts in rib, rib to end. Work on remaining 13(15-17-19) sts as given from ★ to end.

Back

Work exactly as given for Front omitting buttonholes.

Finishing and Borders

Read pressing instructions on ball band.

Front Border: With right side facing, using circular needle and C, pick up and k36(39-42-45) sts evenly up left armhole edge of bib, 13(15-17-19) sts along top edge, 21 sts down left side of neck, 27(27-29-31) sts along front of neck, 21 sts up right side of neck, 13(15-17-19) sts along top edge and 36(39-42-45) sts down right armhole edge. 167(177-189-201) sts.

Knit 1 row. Cast off.

Back Border: Work to match Front Border.

Join side seams to start of bib. Join inside leg and crutch seams. Sew on buttons.

31

Double Breasted Jacket

Measurements

To fit chest sizes

| 45 | 50 | 55 | cm |
| 18 | 20 | 22 | ins |

Finished measurement

| 53 | 57 | 61 | cm |
| 20½ | 22½ | 24½ | ins |

Length to shoulder

| 29 | 31 | 32 | cm |
| 11½ | 12 | 12½ | ins |

Sleeve seam

| 16 | 18 | 20 | cm |
| 6½ | 7 | 8 | ins |

Materials

Double Knitting Yarn
200   200   250   balls
4mm and 3.5mm crochet hooks.
6 buttons.

Tension

20 sts and 12 rows = 10 cm [4 ins] square measured over pattern on larger hook.

Back

Using larger hook make 56(60-64)ch and ★work 1tr into 4th ch from hook, *miss 1ch, 1dc into next ch, miss 1ch, 3tr into next ch; rep from * to last 4ch, miss 1ch, 1dc into next ch, 2tr into last ch, 1ch to turn.

Commence Pattern

1st row: 1dc into first tr, *3tr into next dc, 1dc into centre of 3tr; rep from * to last dc, 3tr into dc, 1dc into top of 2ch at beg of previous row.

2nd row: 2ch (count as 1tr), 1tr into first dc, *1dc into centre of 3tr group, 3tr into next dc; rep from * ending with 2tr into last dc, 1ch to turn. ★ 53(57-61) sts.

These 2 rows form the pattern stitch. Work straight until back measures 29(31-34) cm [11½(12-12½) ins], or required length to shoulders ending with a 2nd(1st-2nd) row of pattern.

Shape Back Neck

Next row: Work 25(27-29) sts in pattern and fasten off.

Miss next 4 complete 3tr groups, rejoin yarn to centre of next 3tr group and work 3tr into next dc, work in pattern to end. Fasten off.

Left Front

Using larger hook make 40(44-44)ch and work as given for Back from ★ to ★. 37(41-41) sts.

Work straight until front is 5(6-6) rows shorter than back to shoulder thus ending at front edge.

Shape Neck

1st row: Sl st across 15 sts, 2ch, 1dc into centre of group, work in pattern to end.

Next row: Work in pattern to last 3tr group, 1dc into centre of group, 1tr into next dc, turn.

Next row: 2ch, 1dc into centre of group, work in pattern to end.

1st and 3rd sizes only

Next row: Work in pattern to last dc, 2tr into dc, turn.

Work 1 row straight. Fasten off.

2nd size only

Next row: Work in pattern to last 3tr group, 1dc into centre of group, 1tr into next dc, turn.

Next row: 2ch, 1tr into first dc, work in pattern to end.

Work 1 row straight. Fasten off.

31

Mark positions for 3 pairs of buttons, the first pair 8(9-11) cm [3(3½-4¼) ins] above cast on edge and the 3rd pair 1 cm [½ inch] below start of neck shaping. Space remaining pair halfway between.

Right Front

Work exactly as given for Left Front but making buttonholes from front edge to match markers as follows: 1ch, 1dc into first tr, 2tr into next dc, 1tr into next tr, 1ch, miss 1tr, 1tr into next tr, 2tr into next dc, 1dc into centre of next 3tr, 3tr into next dc, 1dc into centre of next 3tr, 2tr into next dc, 1tr into next tr, 1ch, miss 1tr, 1tr into next tr, 2tr into next dc, 1dc into centre of next 3tr, work in pattern to end.

When working next row work 3tr into ch space.

Sleeves

Using larger hook make 27(31-31)ch and work as given for Back from ★ to ★. 25(29-29) sts. Work 1(1-3) more rows in pattern.

Bringing extra sts into pattern when possible inc 1 st at each end of next and every alt row until there are 41(45-49) sts. Work straight until sleeve measures approximately 16(18-21) cm [6¼(7-8¼) ins], or required seam length ending with a 2nd row of pattern.

Collar

Using smaller hook make 22ch, work 1dc into 2nd ch from hook, 1dc into each ch to end. 21dc.

Next row: Make 9ch, work 1dc into 2nd ch from hook, 1dc into each ch and each dc across row. 29dc.

Rep the last row 3 times more. 53dc.

Commence Pattern

1st row: 2ch, 1tr into first dc, *miss 1dc, 1dc into next dc, miss 1dc, 3tr into next dc; rep from * ending with 2tr into last dc, 1ch to turn.

Change to larger hook and work 3 rows in pattern as given for Back.

Next row: 2ch, 1dc into centre of group, work in pattern to last 3tr group, 1dc into centre of group, 1tr into last dc, turn.

Rep the last row once more. Fasten off.

Finishing and Edgings

Read pressing instructions on ball band. Join shoulder, side and sleeve seams. Insert sleeves. Sew dc edge of collar to neck edge starting and finishing 5 cm [2 ins] in from each front edge.

Edging: With right side of work facing and using larger hook, join yarn to lower edge of left side seam, work 1 round of firm dc all round outer edge of jacket, working 3dc into each corner, sl st to join, turn.

Next round: Work 1dc into each dc, working 3dc into each corner st, work to end. Sl st to join. Fasten off.

Sleeve Edging: Using larger hook work 2 rounds of firm dc round lower edge of each sleeve. Fasten off.

Press seams. Sew on buttons.

— ◆ —

32/33.

Sweater and Trousers

Measurements

To fit chest sizes

| 40 | 45 | 50 | cm |
| 16 | 18 | 20 | ins |

Sweater

Finished measurement

| 47 | 52 | 57 | cm |
| 19 | 21 | 23 | ins |

Length to shoulder

| 21 | 26 | 30 | cm |
| 8¼ | 10¼ | 12 | ins |

Sleeve length

| 13 | 15 | 17 | cm |
| 5 | 6 | 6¾ | ins |

Trousers

Inside leg seam

| 17 | 21 | 25 | cm |
| 6¾ | 8¼ | 10 | ins |

32/33

Materials

Double Knitting

Sweater
  200   200   200   grams

Trousers
  150   200   200   grams

Pair needles each size 4mm (8) and 3¼mm (10). Cable needle and 2 buttons for sweater. Waist length of 2.5 cm [1 inch] wide elastic for Trousers

Tension

24 sts and 32 rows = 10 cm [4 ins] square measured over double moss stitch using larger needles.

Special Abbreviation

C8B (Cable 8 Back) = slip next 4 sts onto cable needle and hold at back of work, knit next 4 sts from left-hand needle, then knit sts from cable needle.

Sweater

Back

Using smaller needles cast on 54(62-66) sts.

1st row (right side): K2, *p2, k2; rep from * to end.

2nd row: P2, *k2, p2; rep from * to end.

Rep the last 2 rows until rib measures 3(3-4) cm [1¼(1¼-1½) ins] ending with a right side row.

Next row (increase): Rib 5(8-9), inc in each of next 10(9-10) sts, rib 24(28-28), inc in each of next 10(9-10) sts, rib to end. 74(80-86) sts.

Change to larger needles and commence pattern.

1st row: K1, [p1, k1] 1(2-3) times, *p2, k8, p2, k1, p2, k8*, [p1, k1] 10(11-12) times, rep from * to *, p1, [k1, p1] 2(3-4) times.

2nd row: k1, [p1, k1] 2(3-4) times, *p8, k2, p1, k2, p8, k2*, [k1, p1] 10(11-12) times, rep from * to *, p1, [k1, p1] 1(2-3) times.

3rd row: P1, [k1, p1] 2(3-4) times, *k8, p1, [k1, p1] twice, k8, p2* [k1, p1] 10(11-12) times, rep from * to *, k1, [p1, k1] 1(2-3) times.

4th row: P1, [k1, p1] 1(2-3) times, *k2, p8, k1, [p1, k1] twice, p8*, [k1, p1] 10(11-12) times, rep from * to *, k1, [p1, k1] 2(3-4) times.

5th row: K1, [p1, k1] 1(2-3) times, *p2, C8B, p2, k1, p2, C8B*, [p1, k1] 10(11-12) times, rep from * to *, p1, [k1, p1] 2(3-4) times.

6th, 7th and 8th rows: As 2nd 3rd and 4th rows.

These 8 rows form the pattern. Continue in pattern until back measures 21(26-30) cm [8¼(10¼-12) ins] or required length to shoulders ending with a wrong side row.

Shape shoulders

Cast off 27(30-32) sts at beg of next 2 rows. Cast off remaining 20(20-22) sts.

Front

Work as given for Back until front measures 11(12-13) cm [4¼(4¾-5) ins] **less** than back to shoulders ending with a right side row.

Divide for Front Opening

Next row: Work 34(37-40) sts, cast off next 6 sts, work to end.

Continue on these 34(37-40) sts first. ★ Work straight until front is 17(17-19) rows shorter than back to start of shoulder shaping (work 1 more row here for 2nd side), thus ending at neck edge.

Shape Neck

Cast off 2 sts at beg of next row. Dec 1 st at neck edge on next 3 rows, then following 2(2-3) alt rows. 27(30-32) sts remain. Work 9 rows straight, thus ending at side edge. Cast off.

With right side facing rejoin yarn to remaining 34(37-40) sts and complete as given for first side from ★ to end reversing shaping where indicated.

Sleeves

Using smaller needles cast on 30(34-38) sts and work 3(3-4) cm [1¼(1¼-1½) ins] in k2, p2 rib as given for Back ending with a right side row.

Next row (increase): Rib 1(3-5), *inc in each of next 2 sts, work 1 st; rep from * to last 2(4-6) sts, inc in next st, rib to end. 49(53-57) sts.

Change to larger needles and commence double moss st:

1st row: K1, *p1, k1; rep from * to end.

2nd row: P1, *k1, p1; rep from * to end.

3rd row: As 2nd row.

4th row: As 1st row

Rep these 4 rows until sleeve measures 13(15-17) cm [5(6-6¾) ins ending with a wrong side row. Cast off.

Collar

Using smaller needles cast on 70(70-74) sts and work 5(5-6) cm in k2, p2 as rib given for Back ending with a wrong side row. Cast off 7 sts in rib at beg of next 6 rows. Cast off remaining 28(28-32) sts in rib.

Finishing and Bands

Read pressing instructions on ball band.

Left Front Band: Using smaller needles and with right side facing, pick up and k18(18-22) sts along left front edge. Work 7 rows in k2, p2, rib as given for Back starting with the 2nd row. Cast off in rib.

Right Front Band:

Using smaller needles and with right side facing, pick up and k18(18-22) sts along right front edge. Work 3 rows in k2, p2 rib as given for Back starting with the 2nd row.

Next row (buttonholes): K2, p2tog, yon, rib 10(10-14), yfrn, p2tog, k2. Work 3 more rows in rib. Cast off in rib.

Join shoulder seams. Fold sleeves in half lengthways and mark centre of cast off edge. Sew sleeve to side edge placing centre at shoulder seam. **Note:** armhole should measure approximately 10(11-12) cm [4(4¼-4¾) ins]. Join side and sleeve seams. Sew side edges of bands to cast off sts at centre front. Sew shaped edge of collar to neck edge starting and finishing at inner edge of front bands. Sew on buttons.

Trousers

Legs (Make 2)

Using smaller needles cast on 42(46-50) sts and work 3(3-4) cm [1¼(1¼-1½) ins] in k2, p2 rib as given for Back of Sweater ending with a right side row.

Next row (increase): Rib 3(3-4), inc in each st to last 4(4-5) sts, rib to end. 77(85-91) sts.

Change to larger needles and work in double moss st as given for Sleeves of Sweater until leg measures 17(21-25) cm [6¾(8¼-10) ins] ending with a wrong side row.

Shape Crutch

Cast off 3 sts at beg of next 2 rows. Dec 1 st at each end of next 5 rows then following 2(3-3) alt rows. 57(63-69) sts remain. Work straight until piece measures 11(13-15) cm [4¼(5-6) ins measured straight from start of crutch shaping, ending with a wrong side row and decreasing 3(1-3) sts evenly across last row. 54(62-66) sts remain.

Change to smaller needles and work 3 cm in k2, p2 rib as given for Back of Sweater. Cast off loosely in rib.

To Finish

Read pressing instructions on ball band. Join inside leg and crutch seams. Join elastic into a ring, place inside waistband and work a herringbone stitch over elastic onto every alternate stitch of ribbing thus enclosing the elastic.

— ◆ —

34/35

Striped Sweater and Cardigan

Measurements

To Fit Chest sizes

| 40 | 45 | 50 | cm |
| 16 | 18 | 20 | ins |

Finished measurements

| 46 | 52 | 57 | cm |
| 18½ | 21 | 23 | ins |

Length to shoulder

| 22 | 25 | 29 | cm |
| 8¾ | 10 | 11½ | ins |

Sleeve length

| 13 | 15 | 17 | cm |
| 5 | 6 | 6¾ | ins |

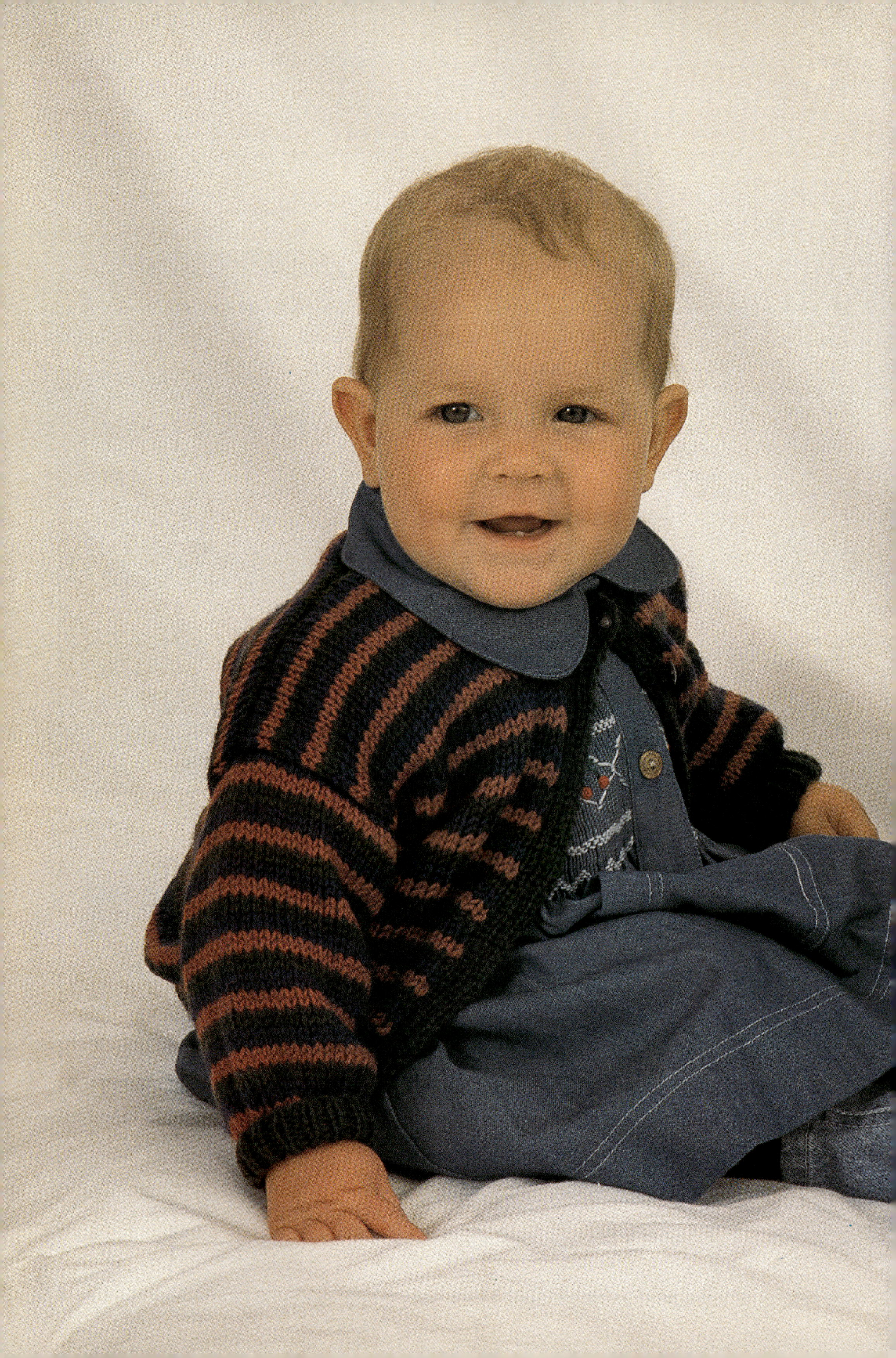

34/35

Materials

Double Knitting Yarn

Sweater or Cardigan

Colour A
50   100   100   balls

Colour B
50   50   50   balls

Colour C
50   50   50   balls

Pair needles each size 3¼mm (10) 4mm (8). 4(4-5) buttons for cardigan.

Tension

22 sts and 30 rows = 10 cm [4 ins] square measured over st st using larger needles.

Sweater
Back

Using smaller needles and A cast on 51(57-63) sts.

1st row (right side): K1, *p1, k1; rep from * to end.

2nd row: P1, *k1, p1; rep from * to end.

Rep the last 2 rows 4(5-5) times more.

Change to larger needles. Working in st st starting knit, work 2 rows in C, 2 rows in B and 2 rows in A. These 6 rows form the stripe pattern ★. Work in pattern until the back measures approximately 22(25-29) cm [8¾10-11½ ins] or required length to shoulder ending with 2 rows in A.

Shape Shoulders

Cast off 17(19-21) sts at beg of next 2 rows. Slip remaining 17(19-21) sts at beg of next 2 rows. Slip remaining 17(19-21) sts onto a holder for neckband.

Tip

Use up your oddments of yarn to knit a sweater or cardigan in random colours. The number of rows in each stripe can vary, however it is advisable to work an even number of rows, so that the colours can be carried up the side of the work.

Sleeves

Using smaller needles and A cast on 31(33-35) sts and work 9(11-11) rows in rib as given for Back.

Next row (increase): Rib 3(1-5), *inc in next st, rib 2(2-1); rep from * to last 4(2-6) sts, inc in next st, rib to end. 40(44-48) sts.

Change to larger needles and work in stripe pattern as given for Back until sleeve measures 13(15-17) cm [5(6-6¾) ins] ending with a purl row. Cast off.

Front

Work as given for Back to ★.

Rep the last 6 rows until front is 15(17-17) rows shorter than Back to start of shoulder shaping, ending with a right side row in B(C-C).

Shape Neck

Work 22(24-26) sts, turn and complete this side first.

Keeping stripe pattern correct dec 1 st at neck edge on next 3 rows, then following 2 alt rows. 17(19-21) sts remain. Work 8(10-10) rows straight (work 1 row less here for 2nd side). Cast off.

Slip next 7(9-11) sts at centre onto a holder. With wrong side facing rejoin B(C-C) to neck edge of remaining 22(24-26) sts and work to end. Complete as given for first side working 1 row less where indicated.

Finishing and Neckband

Read pressing instructions on ball band. Join left shoulder seam.

Neckband: Using smaller needles and A and with right side facing knit across sts at back neck decreasing 1 st at centre, pick up and k14(16-16) sts down left front slope, knit across sts at centre front and pick up and k14(16-16) sts up right front slope. 51(59-63) sts. Work 7 rows in k1, p1 rib as given for Back starting with the 2nd row. Cast off in rib.

Join right shoulder seam leaving neckband and 5 cms [2 ins] of shoulder open. Using A and with right side facing work 1 row of double crochet around opening, then work a 2nd row making 2 button loops evenly spaced on front edge by working 2 chain in place of 1 double crochet. Fasten off.

Mark centre of cast off edge of sleeve. Sew sleeve to side edge above last stripe in C placing centre at shoulder seam. Join side and sleeve seams. Press seams. Sew on buttons.

Cardigan
Back an Sleeves

Work as given for Back and Sleeves of Sweater.

Left Front

Using smaller needles and A cast on 29(33-35) sts and work 9(11-11) rows in rib as given for Back.

Next row: Rib 6, slip these sts onto a safety pin, rib to end increasing 1 st at end of row for 1st size only. 24(27-29) sts remain.

★★ Change to larger needles and work in stripe pattern as given for Back until Front is 15(17-17) rows shorter than back to start of shoulder shaping (work 1 row more here for Right Front), thus ending a front edge in C(C-A).

Shape Neck

Next row: Work 2(3-3) sts, slip these sts onto a safety pin, work to end.

Dec 1 st at neck edge on next 3 rows, then following 2 alt rows. 17(19-21) sts remain. Work 7(7-9) rows straight, thus ending at side edge. Cast off.

Right Front

Using smaller needles and A cast on 29(33-35) sts and work 4 rows in k1, p1 rib as given for Back.

Next row (Buttonhole): Rib 3, yf, k2tog, rib to end. Work 4(6-6) more rows in rib.

Next row: Inc in first st for 1st size only, rib to last 6 sts, turn and slip remaining sts onto a safety pin. 24(27-29) sts remain.

Complete as given for Left Front from ★★ to end, reversing by working 1 row more where indicated.

Finishing and Neckband

Read pressing to instructions on ball band. Join shoulder seam.

Left Front Band: Using smaller

36
Yoked Dress

Measurements
To fit chest sizes

| 40 | 45 | 50 | cm |
| 16 | 18 | 20 | ins. |

Length from back of neck

| 29 | 33 | 38 | cm |
| 11½ | 13 | 15 | ins |

Sleeve seam

| 13 | 15 | 17 | cm |
| 5 | 6 | 6¾ | ins |

Materials
Double Knitting Yarn
Main colour (M)

| 150 | 200 | 250 | grams |

Contrast colour (C)

| 50 | 50 | 50 | grams |

---

needles and A cast on 1 st and with right side of left front facing rib across sts on safety pin. 7 sts. Continue in rib until band, **when slightly stretched,** fits up front edge to start of neck shaping ending with a wrong side row. Break yarn and slip sts onto a safety pin.

Sew band in place stretching evenly and mark positions for 4 buttons, the first to match existing buttonhole in right front welt and allowing for a 5th to be placed 3 rows above sts on safety pin. Space remainder evenly between.

Right Front Band: Work as given for Left Front Band but starting with wrong side of right front facing, **at the same time** making buttonholes to match markers on right side rows as before. Leave sts on needle and do not break yarn at end.

Sew band in place. Join shoulder seams.

Neckband: Continuing on from sts of right front band, knit across sts on safety pin at right front neck, pick up and k13(13-15) sts up right front slope, knit across sts on holder at back neck, pick up and k13(13-15) sts down left front slope, knit across sts on safety pin at left front neck and rib across sts of left front band. 61(65-71) sts.

Starting with a 2nd row, work 5 rows in k1, p1 rib as given for Back, making buttonhole as before on 2nd of these rows. Cast off in rib.

Fold sleeves in half lengthways and mark centre of cast off edge. Sew sleeves to side edges placing centre at shoulder seam. Join side and sleeve seams. Sew on buttons.

Tip
Always join in a new ball of yarn at the start of a row. To make a perfect join at the edge of the work, simply drop the old yarn and start working with the new yarn. after a few stitches, tie the old and new ends in a loose knot. The ends can be darned into the seam at a later stage.

36

Pair needles each size 4mm (8) and 3¾mm (9). Twin pin size 4mm (8) if required. 3 buttons. Shirring elastic if required.

Tension

24 sts and 32 rows to 10 cms [14 ins] measured over st st using larger needles.

Note

You may find it easier to work skirt or yoke on a Twin Pin, turning at end of each row, in order to accommodate the large number of sts.

Skirt

(worked in one piece to armholes)

Using smaller needles and C cast on 168(192-216) sts firmly thumb method, and work 2 rows in garter st (every row knit).

Change to larger needles. Join in M and work 6 rows in st st, starting knit (right side). Using C work 2 more rows in garter st. Break off C and continuing in M only work in st st until skirt measures 21(23-26) cms [8¼(9-10¼) ins], or required length to armholes ending with a purl row.

Divide for Armholes

Next row: K42(48-54), turn and work on these sts first for **Left Back**.

★Work 2(4-8) more rows in st st.

Next row (decrease):*P2tog; rep from * to end ★.

Slip remaining 21(24-27) sts onto a holder for yoke.

With right side of work facing rejoin yarn to next st, k84(96-108), turn and work on these sts for **Front**. Work as given from ★ to ★. Slip remaining 42(48-54) sts onto a holder for yoke.

With right side of work facing rejoin yarn to next st and knit across remaining 42(48-54) sts for **Right Back**. Work as given from ★ to ★.

Slip remaining 21(24-27) sts onto a holder for yoke.

Sleeves

Using smaller needles and C cast on 33(35-37) sts thumb method and work 8 rows in garter st.

Next row (increase): Inc in first st, *k1, inc in next st; rep from * to end. 50(53-56) sts.

Change to larger needles and M and work in st st, starting purl, until sleeve measures 13(15-17) cms [5(6-6¼) ins], or required seam length ending with a purl row. Place a marker at each end of last row to mark end of sleeve seam. Work 3(5-9) more rows.

Next row (decrease): P2(4-5), *p2tog, p2; rep from * to last 4(5-7) sts, p2tog, purl to end.

Slip remaining 38(41-44) sts onto a holder for yoke.

57

Yoke

Using larger needles and C, and with right side of work facing, knit across sts on holders at left back, one sleeve, front, 2nd sleeve and right back. 160(178-196) sts.

Using C knit 1 row. Break off C and join in M.

3rd row (decrease): K7(8-9), *k2tog, k7(8-9); rep from * to end. 143(161-179) sts remain.

4th row: Cast on 2 sts, knit these sts, k3, purl to last 3 sts, k3, turn and cast on 2 sts. 147(165-183) sts.

5th row: Knit to end.

6th row: K5, purl to last 5 sts, k5.

7th row (decrease and buttonhole): K8(9-10), *k2tog, k6(7-8); rep from * to last 11(12-13) sts, k2tog, k6(7-8), yf, k2tog, k1. 130(148-166) sts remain.

8th row: As 6th row.

Join in C and work 2 rows in garter st. Break off C and continue in M only.

11th row (decrease): K8(9-10), *k2tog, k5(6-7); rep from * to last 10(11-12) sts, k2tog, knit to end. 113(131-149) sts remain.

Keeping garter st borders correct and remainder in st st, work 3 rows straight.

15th row (decrease): K7(8-9), *k2tog, k4(5-6); rep from * to last 10(11-12) sts, k2tog, knit to end. 96(114-132) sts remain.

Work 1(3-3) rows straight.

2nd size only

Next row (decrease and buttonhole): k8, *k2tog, k4; rep from * to last 10 sts, k2tog, k5, yf, k2tog, k1. 97 sts remain.

Work 3 rows.

3rd size only

Next row (decrease): k9, *k2tog, k5; rep from * to last 11 sts, k2tog, knit to end 115 sts remain.

Work 1 row.

1st(3rd) sizes only

Next row (buttonhole): knit to last 3 sts, yf, k2tog, k1.

Work 1 row.

All sizes

Next row (decrease): K7(7-8), *k2tog, k3(3-4); rep from * to last 9(10-11) sts, k2tog, knit to end. 79(80-98) sts remain.

Work 1(1-3) rows.

Next row (decrease): K6(7-8), *k2tog, k2(2-3); rep from * to last 9(9-10) sts, k2tog, knit to end. 62(63-81) sts remain.

3rd size only

Work 1 row.

Next row (decrease): K7, *k2tog, k2; rep from * to last 10 sts, k2tog, knit to end. 64 sts remain.

All sizes

Work 1 row. Change to smaller needles and C and work 9 rows in garter st, making buttonhole as before on 5th of these rows. Cast off knitwise.

To Finish

Read pressing instructions on ball band. Join back seam to cast on sts of bands. Join sleeve seams to markers. Join underarm seams. Sew cast on sts of bands in place. Press seams. Sew on buttons. Using C embroider as illustrated if required. Thread shirring elastic through cuffs if required.

37/38.

Motif Sweater and Trousers

Measurements

To fit chest size

| 40 | 45 | 50 | 55 | cm |
| 16 | 18 | 20 | 22 | ins |

Sweater
Finished Measurement

| 46 | 52 | 57 | 61 | cm |
| 18½ | 21 | 23 | 24½ | ins |

Length to shoulder

| 22 | 26 | 30 | 35 | cm |
| 8¾ | 10½ | 12 | 14 | ins |

Sleeve length

| 13 | 15 | 18 | 21 | cm |
| 5¼ | 6 | 7¼ | 8½ | ins |

Trousers
Leg length

| 17 | 21 | 25 | 32 | cm |
| 6¾ | 8½ | 10 | 12¾ | ins |

Length from crotch to waist

| 14 | 16 | 18 | 20 | cm |
| 5½ | 6½ | 7¼ | 8 | ins |

Materials

Double Knitting Yarn

Sweater
Main colour (M)
  100 100 150 150 grams
Contrast colour A
  25 25 25 25 grams
Oddment in Contrast colour B

Trousers (one colour)
  100 150 150 200 grams

Pair of knitting needles each size 3¼ mm (10) and 4 mm (8). 3 buttons for Sweater. Oddments of fine black yarn for eyes. Waist length 2 cm [¾ inch] wide elastic for Trousers.

Tension

22 sts and 30 rows = 10 cm [4 ins] measured over stocking stitch using larger needles.

Special Abbreviations

M1 (make 1) = pick up horizontal loop before next st and work into back of it.

Slip marker = make a slip knot in a short length of contrasting yarn and place on needle where indicated. On following rows slip marker from one needle to the other until chart is completed.

Sweater

Front

Using smaller needles and M cast on 51(57-63-67) sts.

37/38

1st row (right side): K1, *p1, k1; rep from * to end.

2nd row: P1, *k1, p1; rep from * to end.

Rep the last 2 rows 4(4-5-5) times more.

Change to larger needles and work 1(5-11-17) rows in st st, starting knit.

Next row: P12(15-18-20)M, slip marker, work 1st row of chart 1 across next 27 sts, slip marker, p12(15-18-20)M.

Next row: K12(15-18-20)M, work 2nd row of chart k12(15-18-20)M.

These 2 rows form the st st either side of chart. Keep chart correct until completed, then cont in M only, **at the same time** work 36(42-46-52) more rows straight, thus ending with a right side row.

★ **Shape Neck**

Next row: P22(24-27-29), turn and complete this side first.

Dec 1 st at neck edge on next 3 rows, then foll 2(2-2-3) alt rows. 17(19-22-23) sts remain. Work 9(11-11-11) rows straight, thus ending with a wrong side row. Cast off.

Slip next 7(9-9-9) sts at centre onto a holder. With wrong side facing rejoin yarn to remaining 22(24-27-29) sts and purl to end.

Dec 1 st at neck edge on next 3 rows, then foll 2(2-2-3) alt rows. 17(19-22-23) sts remain. Work 1(3-3-3) rows straight, thus ending with a wrong side row. Cast off ★.

Back

Work as given for Front, omitting motif, until back measures same as right front to shoulder, ending with a purl row.

Shape Shoulders

Next row: Cast off 17(19-22-23) sts, knit until there are 17(19-19-21) sts on right-hand needle, cast off remaining 17(19-22-23) sts.

Slip remaining sts onto a holder.

Sleeves

Using smaller needles and M cast on 31(33-35-37) sts and work 9(9-11-11) rows in k1, p1 rib as given for Front.

Next row (increase): Rib 2(5-4-3), *M1, rib 3(2-2-2); rep from * to last 2(6-5-4) sts, M1, rib to end. 41(45-49-53) sts.

Change to larger needles and work in st st, starting knit, until sleeve measures 13(15-18-21) cm [5(6-7-8¼) ins] or required length, ending with a purl row. Cast off.

Finishing and Bands

Read pressing instructions on ball band. Join right shoulder seam.

Neckband: Using smaller needles and M and with right side facing, pick up and k8(10-10-12) sts down left front slope, knit across sts at centre, pick up and k16(18-18-20) sts up right front slope and knit across sts at back neck decreasing 1 st at centre. 47(55-55-61) sts.

Work 8 rows in k1, p1 rib. Cast off in rib.

Button Band: Using smaller needles and M and with right side facing, pick up and k27(29-31-33) sts evenly along left back shoulder including neckband.

Work 8 rows in k1, p1 rib, starting with the 2nd row. Cast off in rib.

Buttonhole Band: Using smaller needles and M and with right side facing, pick up and k27(29-31-33) sts evenly down along left front shoulder including neckband.

Work 3 rows in k1, p1 rib, starting with the 2nd row.

Buttonhole row: Rib 4, [cast off next 2 sts, rib until there are 7(8-9-10) sts on right-hand needle after casting

■ = M   □ = A   ⊠ = B

Read odd number (knit) rows from right to left and even number (purl) rows from left to right. Use separate balls of yarn for each block of colour, twisting yarns together on wrong side of work when changing colour to avoid making a hole.

Tip

For very small areas of colour, you may find it easier and neater to swiss darn (or duplicate) the stitches rather than knitting them in (see page 4).

To Finish

Read pressing instructions on ball band.

Join inside leg and crotch seams. Join elastic into a ring and place inside waistband. Work a herringbone st over the elastic onto every alternate st of ribbing, thus enclosing the elastic.

— ◆ —

39-41

T-Shirt, Knee Pants and Socks

off] twice, cast off next 2 sts, rib to end.

Work 4 more rows in rib, casting on 2 sts over each buttonhole on first of these rows. Cast off in rib.

Embroider details following chart. Lay buttonhole band over button band and tack together at side edge. Fold sleeves in half lengthways and mark centre of cast off edge. Sew sleeve to side edge, placing centre at right shoulder seam or **top** of buttonhole band, and working through double thickness of bands. **Note:** armhole should measure approximately 9(10-11-12) cm. Join side and sleeve seams. Sew on buttons.

Trousers

Legs (Both alike)

Using smaller needles cast on 37(39-43-47) sts and work 11(11-13-13) rows in k1, p1 rib as given for Front of Sweater.

Next row (increase:) Rib 3(1-1-3), *M1, k1, M1, p1; rep from * to end. 71(77-85-91) sts.

Change to larger needles and work in st st, starting knit, until leg measures 17(21-25-32) cm [6¾(8¼-10-12½) ins] or required length, ending with a purl row.

Shape Crotch

Cast off 4(4-5-5) sts at beg of next 2 rows. Dec 1 st at each end of next 5 rows. 53(59-65-71) sts remain. Work straight until crotch measures 11(13-15-17) cm [4¼(5-6-6¾) ins], measured straight from start of crotch shaping and ending with a purl row.

Change to smaller needles and knit 1 row. Work 8 rows in k1, p1 rib as given for Front of Sweater, starting with the 2nd row. Cast off in rib.

Measurements

To fit chest sizes

| 45 | 50 | 55 | cm |
| 18 | 20 | 22 | ins |

T-Shirt

Finished measurement

| 51 | 57 | 62 | cm |
| 20½ | 23 | 25 | ins |

Full length

| 22 | 24 | 26 | cm |
| 8½ | 9½ | 10¼ | ins |

Knee Pants

Inside leg seam

| 13 | 16 | 19 | cm |
| 5 | 6¼ | 7½ | ins |

Socks

Foot length

| 9 | 10 | 11 | cm |
| 3½ | 4 | 4½ | ins |

61

Materials

4 ply Knitting Yarn
T-Shirt
Main colour (M)
  50   50   50   grams
Each in contrast colours A and B
  25   25   25   grams

Knee Pants
Main colour (M)
  100   100   100   grams
Each in contrast colours A and B
  25   25   25   grams

Socks
Main colour (M)
  25   25   50   grams
Oddment each in contrast colours A and B

Pair of needles each size 3¼mm (10) and 2¾mm (11). 2 Buttons for T-Shirt. Waist length 2 cm [¾ in] wide elastic for Knee Pants.

Tension

28 sts and 36 rows = 10 cm [4 ins] square measured over st st using larger needles.

30 sts and 32 rows = 10 cm [4 ins] square measured over fairisle pattern using larger needles.

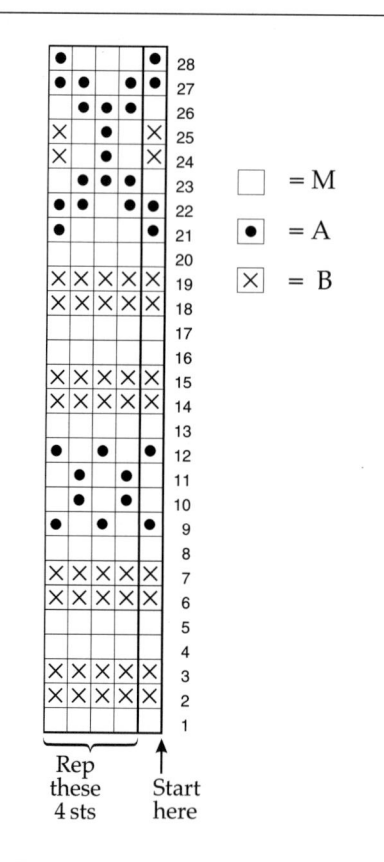

□ = M
● = A
☒ = B

Rep these 4 sts ↑ Start here

Do not weave yarn in at back of work. Carry colour not in use loosely across back of work, or up side edge of work. Read every row from right to left.

T-Shirt
Back

Using smaller needles and M cast on 72(79-87) sts thumb method and work 9 rows in garter st (every row knit - first row is right side).

Next row (increase): K5(4-5), *inc in next st, k14(13-14); rep from * to last 7(5-7) sts, inc in next st, knit to end. 77(85-93) sts.

Change to larger needles. Working in st st, starting knit, and joining in A and B when required, work the 28 rows of Chart until back measures 13(14-15) cm [5(5½-6) ins], or required length to underarms ending with a purl row.

Shape Sleeves

Keeping pattern correct and bringing extra sts into pattern cast on 8(12-12) sts at beg of next 2 rows. 93(109-117) sts ★.

Work straight until sleeves measure 5(6-7) cm [2(2½-2¾) ins] from cast on sts ending with a knit row.

Divide for Opening

Next row: Keeping pattern correct work 44(52-56) sts, turn and complete this side first.

Work straight until sleeve measures 9(10-11) cm [3½(4-4½) ins] from cast on sts ending with a knit row.

Next row: Cast off 30(37-40) sts, purl to end.

Break yarn and slip remaining 14(15-16) sts onto a holder for neckband.

Slip next 5 sts at centre onto a safety pin for buttonhole band. With wrong side of work facing rejoin yarn to remaining sts and work in pattern to end. 44(52-56) sts.

Work straight until sleeve measures 9(10-11) cm [3½(4-4½) ins] from cast on sts ending with a purl row.

Next row: Cast off 30(37-42) sts, knit to end.

Purl 1 row. Break yarn and slip remaining 14(15-16) sts onto a holder for neckband.

Front

Work as given for the Back to ★. Work straight until sleeves measure 4(5-5) cm [1½(2-2) ins] from cast on sts, ending with a knit row.

Shape Neck

Next row: Keeping pattern correct p35(42-45), turn and complete this side.

★★Dec 1 st at neck edge on next 3 rows, then following 2 alt rows. 30(37-40) sts remain. Work straight until front measures same as back to shoulder ending at sleeve edge. Cast off.

Slip next 23(25-27) sts at centre onto a holder for neckband. With wrong side of work facing rejoin yarn to neck edge of remaining sts and purl to end. 35(42-45) sts. Complete as given for first side from ★★ to end.

To Finish

Read pressing instructions on ball band.

Buttonhole Band

Using smaller needles and M cast on 1 st and with right side of work facing knit across sts on safety pin at division for opening. 6 sts. Work 5 rows in garter st.

Next row (Buttonhole): Knit to last 4 sts, yf, k2tog, k2.

Continue in garter st until band, **when slightly stretched,** fits up back opening ending with a wrong side row. Break yarn and slip sts onto a saftey pin for neckband.

Button Band

Using smaller needles and M cast on 6 sts and work in garter st until band, **when slightly stretched,** fits up back opening ending with a right side row. Leave sts on needle and do not break yarn.

Join shoulder seams.

Neckband

Continuing on from sts of button band knit across sts on holder at left back neck decreasing 1 st at centre, pick up and k13(15-17) sts down left front slope, work across sts on holder at front neck as follows: k3(4-5), [k2tog, k3] 3 times, k2tog, knit to end pick up and k13(15-17) sts up right front slope, then knit across sts at right back neck and buttonhole band. 81(89-97) sts.

Work 8 rows in garter st, **at the same time** making buttonhole as before on 4th of these rows. Cast off knitwise.

39-41

Sleeve Edgings (Both alike)

Using smaller needles and M with right side of work facing, pick up and k50(56-62) sts evenly along one sleeve edge. Work 8 rows in garter st. Cast off knitwise.

Join side and underarm seams. Sew button and buttonhole bands in place stretching evenly. Sew cast on sts of button band in place. Press seams. Sew on buttons.

Knee Pants
Right Leg

Using smaller needles and M cast on 82(86-90) sts thumb method and work 9 rows in garter st (every row knit - first row is right side).

Next row (increase): K4(6-5), * inc in next st, k11(11-12); rep from * to last 6(8-7) sts, inc in next st, knit to end. 89(93-97) sts.

Change to larger needles. Working in st st, starting knit, and starting with the 13th row, work 23 rows of chart **at the same time** increasing 1 st at each end of 3rd and every following 5th row until there are 99(103-107) sts, thus ending with the 7th row of chart. Break off A and B and continue in M only.

Next row (decrease): P6(8-7), *p2tog, p15(15-11); rep from * to last 8(10-9) sts, p2tog, purl to end. 93(97-99) sts remain.

Work 2 rows straight. Inc 1 st at each end of next and every following 4th row 2(4-7) times in all. 97(105-113) sts.

Work straight until leg measures 13(16-19) cm [5(6¼-7½) ins] or required length ending with a purl row ★.

Shape Crutch

Cast off 4(5-5) sts at beg of next row and 6(7-7) sts at beg of following row. Dec 1 st at each end of next 5 rows, then following 3 alt rows. 71(77-87) sts remain. Purl 1 row. Dec 1 st at end (back edge) of next and following alt row. 69(75-83) sts remain.

★★Work straight until piece measures 13(15-17) cm [5(6-6½) ins] measured straight from start of crutch shaping and ending with a purl row.

Change to smaller needles and commence rib.

1st row: K1, *p1, k1; rep from * to end.

2nd row: P1, *k1, p1; rep from * to end.

Rep the last 2 rows until rib measures 4 cm [1½ ins] ending with a 2nd row. Cast off in rib.

Left Leg

Work as given for Right Leg to ★.

Shape Crutch

Cast off 6(7-7) sts at beg of next row and 4(5-5) sts at beg of following row. Dec 1 st at each end of next 5 rows, then following 3 alt rows. 71(77-87) sts remain. Purl 1 row. Dec 1 st at beg (back edge) of next and following alt row. 69(75-83) sts remain.

Complete as given for Right Leg from ★★ to end.

To Finish

Read pressing instructions on ball band.

Join inside leg and crutch seams. Join elastic into a ring and place inside waistband. Work a herringbone stitch over elastic onto every alt stitch of ribbing thus enclosing the elastic. Press seams.

Socks

Using smaller needles and M cast on 38(42-46) sts thumb method and work 9 rows in garter st (every row knit - first row is right side).

Next row (increase): K4(5-6), * inc in next st, k13(14-15); rep from * to last 6(7-8) sts, inc in next st, knit to end. 41(45-49) sts.

Change to larger needles. Working in st st, starting knit, and starting with the 13th row, work 23 rows of chart, thus ending with the 7th row of chart. Break off A and B and continue in M only.

Next row (decrease): P4(5-6), *p2tog, p13(14-15); rep from * to last 7(8-9) sts, p2tog, purl to end. 38(42-46) sts remain. Break yarn.

Divide for Heel

Slip first 12(13-14) sts onto a holder for heel. Slip next 14(16-18) sts onto a holder for instep. Rejoin yarn and knit remaining 12(13-14) sts, then knit across 12(13-14) sts on first holder, turn and work on these 24(26-28) sts for heel.

Work 7(9-11) rows in st st, starting purl.

Turn Heel

1st row: K17(19-21), sl 1, k1, psso, turn.

2nd row: Sl 1, p10(12-14), p2tog, turn.

3rd row: Sl 1, k10(12-14), sl 1, k1, psso, turn.

Rep 2nd and 3rd rows 4 times more, then work 2nd row again. 12(14-16) sts remain.

Next row: Sl 1, knit to end.

Next row: Purl.

Break yarn. With right side of work facing rejoin yarn and pick up and k8(9-10) sts along first side of heel, knit across the 12(14-16) sts on needle, then pick up and k8(9-10) sts along 2nd side of heel. 28(32-36) sts.

Shape Sole

1st row: Purl.

2nd row: K1, sl 1, k1, psso, knit to last 3 sts, k2tog, k1.

Rep the last 2 rows until 14(16-18) sts remain. Work 5(7-7) rows straight, thus ending with a purl row.

★ Shape Toe

1st row: K1, sl 1, k1, psso, knit to last 3 sts, k2tog, k1.

2nd row: P1, p2tog, purl to last 3 sts, p2tog tbl, p1.

3rd row: As 1st row. 8(10-12) sts remain.

4th row: Purl ★.

Break yarn and slip sts onto a double pointed needle.

Instep

With right side of work facing rejoin yarn and knit across sts on holder for instep. 14(16-18) sts. Work straight until instep measures same as sole to start of toe shaping ending with a purl row. Work as given for Toe from ★ to ★. Do not break yarn. With right sides together cast off the 2 sets of sts as follows: *knit tog 1 st from each needle; rep from * once more (2 sts on right-hand needle), pass first st over 2nd to cast off. Continue until all sts are cast off.

To Finish

Read pressing instructions on ball band. Join back and foot seams.